THE STEAMER COOKBOOK

Coleen Simmons
Bob Simmons

BRISTOL PUBLISHING ENTERPRISES
San Leandro, California

A NITTY GRITTY® COOKBOOK

Printed in the United States of America.

ISBN 1-55867-080-7

Cover design: Frank Paredes
Cover photography: John Benson
Food stylist: Suzanne Carreiro
Illustrator: James Balkovek

CONTENTS

INTRODUCTION TO STEAMING: EQUIPMENT; TECHNIQUES

Steaming, one of the oldest methods of food preparation, is becoming increasingly popular in the health-conscious '90s. Steamed foods retain nutrients, color, texture and flavor, without adding calories, fat or sodium, making steaming an ideal cooking method for those on restricted diets.

One usually thinks of vegetables and fish when using the steaming process because little or no seasoning is required to savor their natural flavors and freshness. Meats and poultry also fare well with steaming, staying tender and moist while giving up some of their fat during the cooking process. Duck particularly benefits from being steamed. Steamed sweet puddings have been traditional favorites in Europe and North America for hundreds of years. The Asian community has a large repertoire of delicious snack buns and dumplings that are steamed to perfection.

Steaming is a very economical cooking method utilizing one heat source for a large pot. Several layers can be added to steam under one lid at the same time. It isn't usually necessary to stir foods while they steam, and since foods don't stick and burn, cleanup is very easy.

We have included recipes for breakfast, lunch, dinner and snack foods that can be prepared in a steamer. Many dishes are low calorie and low in fat, but our primary goal was to develop recipes that taste good. Often we recommend a sauce or dressing for a steamed dish to improve the appearance or add flavor.

EQUIPMENT FOR STEAMING

Almost any pan with a lid can be turned into a steamer suitable for steaming one or two portions of steamed vegetables. All that is necessary is an inexpensive collapsible steamer basket. Larger pans with well fitting lids can be adapted to accommodate larger portions. Rig some kind of platform to hold a rack or plate well above the rapidly boiling water. Platforms can be adapted from all kinds of articles readily available in the kitchen. An empty can with both ends cut out will support a steamer plate. An inverted sieve or colander works well. In a roasting pan, use two or three cans to support a large plate when you steam a whole duck or large fish.

If the rack or plate that you are going to use to hold the food doesn't have holes or perforations, make sure that there is at least ½-inch clearance all around between it and the side of the vessel to allow steam circulation.

An inexpensive steamer that works extremely well for us is imported from China. It is made of aluminum and comes in several sizes. Ours is about 12 inches (30 cm) across the top and has two steamer baskets, each about 5 inches high. A domed lid allows steaming whole chickens or other large items. It is possible to cook pasta in the large bottom pot of boiling water while steaming vegetables or other items for the pasta sauce. It is one of the most efficient steamers because the well fitting lid does not allow steam to escape. This is an essential item in an Asian kitchen, so look for one in a Chinese or Vietnamese market.

Chinese bamboo steamers work well, and stack easily. They are designed for use in a wok, but can be adapted to other pans. One drawback is that bamboo steamers tend to mold if they are not carefully dried and stored in a dry airy place. They tend to impart a slight woody flavor to food until they have been used several times so you should boil a new steamer basket in a large pot of water for 10 minutes before using the first time. The bamboo lid permits some of the steam to escape so there is less liquid to moisten the food.

The Yunnan pot is a special clay pot with a lid that is made to sit on top of a medium size saucepan. There is a conical steam vent in the middle that allows steam to circulate around the food being cooked. Yunnan pots make great stews and do a very good job on vegetables. They are limited to steaming small quantities of food. One usually does not need to add any extra broth or liquid to the foods in the pot because a lot of juice is generated during the steaming process.

ELECTRIC STEAMERS

There is a variety of electric steamers now available. Some are small and are designed to cook one layer of food at a time. This type is ideal for steaming vegetables, or making steamed rice for one or two, and works well for small portions of fish and fowl. Some electric steamers have a deep-sided container plus a perforated steaming rack for more cooking versatility.

Larger electric steamers are very useful in making "stacked meals" (see ideas for stacked meals beginning on page 164). The main course, a vegetable and a starch can all be steamed together. The layers are added at the appropriate time to allow the whole meal to be ready at once.

An electric rice cooker makes a good steamer and often comes equipped with a steamer plate. Just be sure to add enough water to assure that the food is cooked before the cooker shuts off. Here again, size is a limitation. The rice cooker boils the liquid very rapidly and there is no way of regulating it during the cooking process.

USEFUL TIPS

Safety cannot be stressed enough! The steam that is hot enough to cook your food is also hot enough to cook you! Always approach a steaming pot with great respect. Keep handy a long oven mitt that comes well up the arm, and use it each time that you remove the steamer lid, or lift out food from the steamer. When removing the steamer lid, always tilt it slowly away from you, and keep your face well back from the steamer. If using an electric steamer, keep it back from the edge of the counter, and make sure that the electric cord doesn't dangle over the edge of the counter where it can be pulled off by a child or the brush of an apron. If you are using multiple steaming baskets, place a cookie sheet with sides or other large heatproof platter near the steamer so you have a place to put down the baskets when you switch them, or check the doneness of the food. A plate lifter is very handy to help lift hot plates from the steamer. Several varieties are available, and they are quite inexpensive.

Each time you open a steamer of any type all the steam will rise and be replaced by cool air. After the cover is replaced it takes a minute or two to build up "a full head of steam." Add that minute to the cooking time.

All cooking times in this book are educated guesses. They are the times that worked well for us when we tested the recipes. It is suggested that you use a thermometer to check the progress of meat and poultry during the cooking.

Several factors can influence the cooking time for any recipe, including:

- The source of heat. How much steam can be generated?

- The fit of the cover on your steamer. Can the steam easily escape?

- The freshness or tenderness of ingredients.

- The amount of food that you are steaming. How thick is the steamed item? Is it a single or double layer?

- Your personal preference for doneness. This varies widely for vegetables, but also somewhat for meat.

- Covering the dish or plate of food being steamed with plastic wrap, foil, or an inverted plate lengthens steaming time.

For dishes requiring longer cooking times, be sure to check the water level frequently. Add boiling water, or add a few minutes to the cooking time to allow the added water to return to a full boil.

For easy cleanup, use nonstick cooking spray on plates to be used in the steamer before you place fish, chicken or meat on them. Consider lining bamboo or aluminum steamer racks with large lettuce, Swiss chard or even grape leaves before adding fish or chicken pieces. Leave at least a 1-inch edge uncovered for steam circulation. Large green leaves can also be placed on top of food to be steamed to add extra flavor and keep off some of the steaming liquid dripping from the lid. Another trick is to invert a slightly larger diameter plate over the bottom plate containing the chicken or fish to keep condensing moisture from diluting the dish.

When steaming breads or cakes, wrap the lid of the steamer with a dish towel to keep the liquid from dripping on the bread. Lay a small piece of parchment paper or aluminum foil over the bread if it is not possible to wrap the steamer lid with a towel.

The steamer is a great kitchen tool. Many delicious, healthful meals can be prepared in it with a minimum of time and effort. Use these recipes for ideas and techniques, and then devise your own favorites. Full steam ahead!

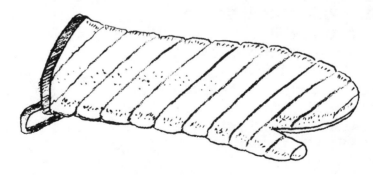

VEGETABLES A-Z

Steaming is one of the best preparations for vegetables because it retains the vegetable's vibrant color and enhances natural fresh flavors. Steaming does not require the addition of any butter, oil or salt, producing very healthy and low calorie dishes. Steaming also allows you to achieve the desired texture of the vegetable. Short steaming times produce tender-crisp asparagus, beans, broccoli and summer squash. Longer steaming is needed for artichokes, beets, chestnuts and spaghetti squash. Be sure to steam potatoes that you are going to use in a potato salad because they hold together so well when they are sliced. Steamed artichokes have an excellent texture without being waterlogged.

There are many suggestions in this section for vegetable toppings, salad dressings and sauces. Try *Cauliflower Calcutta* with its savory cumin and coriander sauce, or spaghetti squash with *Arugula Pesto*, or a *Scallop and Red Pepper Sauce*. Or make *Russian Vegetable Salad* with steamed carrots, potato, celery root and green beans.

The *Spicy Eggplant Appetizer* and *Eggplant Sesame Dip* are great low calorie party dishes because the eggplant is steamed without any fat and then combined with savory spices. Steaming is a great way to prepare stuffed mushrooms for a hot appetizer. We have also included an easy no-stir method for preparing the traditional long-cooking polenta.

ARTICHOKES

Steaming is one of the best ways to cook artichokes and results in a perfect texture with no excess moisture to drain.

1 large trimmed artichoke per person
3-4 cups water, depending on size of steamer

Wash artichokes. Cut off artichoke stem and remove top ¼ of artichoke by cutting leaves straight across the top. Pull off 2 or 3 layers of outer leaves. Trim remaining uncut leaves straight across with scissors. Trim rough edges of artichoke bottoms where leaves were removed.

Add water to steamer and place artichokes stem up on steamer rack. Cover steamer, bring water to a rapid boil and cook 35 to 45 minutes, depending on size. Artichokes are done when bottom is easily pierced with a knife. Remove to a serving platter.

Serve artichokes warm or at room temperature with mayonnaise, melted butter or your favorite sauce.

STEAMED BABY ARTICHOKES

Small steamed artichokes are delicious marinated and served as part of an antipasto plate or added to salads. Choose the smallest ones available.

8-10 small trimmed artichokes
3 cups water

Wash artichokes. Cut off artichoke stem and remove top 1/4 of artichoke by cutting leaves straight across the top. Pull off tough outer leaves. Trim remaining uncut leaves straight across with scissors. Trim rough edges of artichoke bottoms where leaves were removed. Place in steamer basket. Steam over high heat for 12 to 15 minutes, depending on size of artichokes. Artichokes are done when the bottom can easily be pierced with a sharp knife. Remove and allow to cool. Cut each artichoke in half and scoop out prickly centers with a small spoon.

MARINATED BABY ARTICHOKES

These are delicious in the lunch box or as part of an antipasto platter.

8-10 steamed baby artichokes
2 tbs. full-flavored olive oil
1 large clove garlic, minced
1 tbs. lemon juice
1 tbs. rice wine vinegar
¼ tsp. sugar
pinch of sweet basil and oregano
dash red pepper flakes
salt and freshly ground pepper

Cut steamed artichokes in quarters and place in a shallow dish. Heat olive oil in a small skillet and cook garlic over low heat 1 to 2 minutes. Add remaining ingredients, bring to a boil and simmer for 1 to 2 minutes. Pour hot marinade over artichoke halves. Toss to coat with marinade. Cool. Refrigerate until ready to serve.

ASPARAGUS

Asparagus steams quickly and keeps its bright green color. We like to peel the stems for more tender spears. If you have any left over, cover with a little vinaigrette, add some toasted walnuts and serve on tender lettuce leaves for a quick salad course.

1 lb. asparagus, stems trimmed
1 cup water

Place water in steamer. Arrange asparagus spears in steamer basket and place in steamer. Cover steamer. When water comes to a rapid boil, time asparagus for about 8 minutes, or until asparagus is cooked to desired tenderness.

Dress asparagus with a little butter, salt and pepper, or a squeeze of lemon juice, and serve immediately. For use in a salad, run cold water over cooked spears, blot on paper towels, and then add salad dressing.

GREEN BEANS

Both the Romano flat green beans and Blue Lake beans have a nice texture when steamed. A collapsible steamer basket is great for holding the beans.

1 lb. green or Romano beans, stemmed
1-2 cups water

Place water and beans in steamer, cover, and steam for about 10 to 12 minutes after water has come to a boil. Season with salt, pepper and butter to serve warm, or allow to cool and use for a salad. See *Salmon Salad Niçoise*, page 52.

VARIATIONS

- Sauté 2 tbs. slivered or sliced almonds in 2 tbs. butter until lightly browned. Pour over beans and serve immediately.

- Sauté 1 cup thinly sliced mushrooms and 4 minced green onions in 2 tbs. butter. Season with salt and pepper and pour over beans. Serve immediately.

STEAMED BEETS

Small beets are delicious steamed and retain their vibrant color. Try steaming small red and orange beets together to make a colorful side dish.

Wash beets carefully without puncturing skin. Cut off all but about 2 inches of top stem and leave root end intact. Place beets on a collapsible steamer basket or steamer rack. Fresh beets 1½ to 2 inches in diameter will steam in about 40 minutes. When beets are tender, remove to a plate and allow to cool. Peel beets, cut off tops and root ends, and slice.

Serve hot with salt, pepper, butter and a squeeze of lemon juice, or dress with a vinaigrette and serve in a salad.

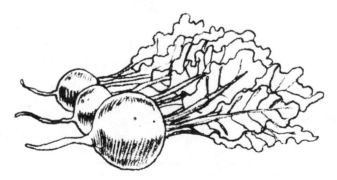

BROCCOLI WITH ORANGE SAUCE

Servings: 4-5

*Here is a quick, flavorful sauce for broccoli or asparagus. Heat the sauce ingredients while the broccoli is steaming and then toss with the broccoli. Add some toasted slivered almonds or pine nuts for a special touch. This is particularly good with **Steamed Mushroom Beef**, page 104.*

1 bunch broccoli florets, steamed

ORANGE SAUCE
1 tbs. butter
2 tbs. orange juice concentrate
½ tsp. finely minced fresh ginger root
1 tbs. soy sauce
salt and white pepper

Steam broccoli for 12 to 15 minutes after water comes to a boil. Just before broccoli is done, heat remaining ingredients in a medium skillet and bring to a boil. When broccoli is steamed to desired tenderness, pour into skillet and toss with orange sauce. Heat through and serve immediately.

STEAMED BRUSSELS SPROUTS

Steaming is one of the best ways to prepare Brussels sprouts, and they make a delicious addition to the holiday table. Brussels sprouts tend to develop a strong cabbage flavor if stored too long after picking.

Prepare sprouts by removing any damaged outer leaves. Trim bottom stem and cut a small cross in it. Place trimmed spouts in steamer basket. When water comes to a boil, steam for about 10 to 12 minutes. Vegetables are done when stem end can be pierced with tip of a knife blade. Toss with butter, salt and pepper, or sprinkle with grated Parmesan cheese.

Steamed Brussels sprouts can be marinated in a light vinaigrette and served as part of an aioli or antipasto platter.

CAULIFLOWER CALCUTTA

Servings: 3-4

*Cauliflower is steamed, tossed with a spicy golden sauce and garnished with fresh cilantro leaves and tomato pieces. This may be served warm or at room temperature. Steamed cauliflower is also delicious with **Lime Jalapeño Butter**, page 25.*

1 head cauliflower separated into florets

SAUCE
2 tbs. butter
½ cup onions, finely chopped
2 cloves garlic, minced
dash red pepper flakes
½ tsp. grated fresh ginger root
1 tsp. cumin

1 tsp. ground coriander
¼ tsp. tumeric
½ cup fresh cilantro leaves for garnish
1 medium tomato, peeled, seeded and chopped for garnish

Steam cauliflower pieces 5 to 8 minutes, depending on size and tenderness you prefer.

Melt butter in a small skillet; sauté onion 3 to 4 minutes until softened. Add remaining ingredients except fresh cilantro leaves and continue to cook over low heat another 2 to 3 minutes. Pour steamed cauliflower into skillet and toss with sauce. Garnish with fresh cilantro and tomato pieces.

CELERY ROOT

This aromatic root vegetable is good raw, blanched or steamed. It is delicious when cooked and pureed with an equal amount of cooked potato, tart apple or carrot. Buy the smaller knobs because the larger ones can have a woody, hollow center.

Cut off top and bottom of celery root and peel rough skin from sides with a sharp knife. Slice into ¼-inch slices and steam for about 10 to 12 minutes, depending on thickness of celery root. Use in *Russian Vegetable Salad*, page 21, or steam with chestnuts to make *Chestnut and Celery Root Puree*, page 24.

RUSSIAN VEGETABLE SALAD

This simple vegetable salad is a great addition to a cold buffet table or served as a side dish for grilled chicken or meat. For an attractive variation, present this salad in hollowed-out tomato cups.

3-4 large carrots, about 10 ozs.
1 large red potato, about 10 ozs.
1 medium celery root
8-10 ozs. green beans or 1 pkg.
   frozen green peas, defrosted

parsley, minced, for garnish
salt and freshly ground pepper
1 tsp. Dijon mustard
½ cup *Easy Mayonnaise* dressing

Peel vegetables and slice potatoes and celery root in ¼-inch thick slices. Slice carrots lengthwise into ¼-inch pieces. Stem green beans and steam whole. When water in steamer comes to a boil, place steamer baskets with vegetable slices over water. Cover and steam for about 10 minutes or until vegetables are tender. Remove vegetables from steamer and refresh in cold water. Let drain and pat dry. Dice vegetables into ½-inch pieces. Add Dijon mustard to mayonnaise, generously salt and pepper vegetables and toss with mustard mayonnaise mixture. Serve immediately, or chill for 1 to 2 hours in the refrigerator before serving.

EASY MAYONNAISE

Make this dressing in the food processor. It is a delicious with fresh cooked crab or shrimp, or use it for sandwiches. It keeps for 4 or 5 days in the refrigerator.

1 large egg
1 tsp. lemon juice
2 tsp. white wine vinegar
1 tsp. Dijon mustard

¼ tsp. salt
generous grind of white pepper
dash Tabasco Sauce
¾ cup vegetable oil

Place egg, lemon juice, wine vinegar, mustard, salt, pepper and Tabasco in the food processor bowl with the metal blade. Cover and process 10 seconds to blend. With motor running, slowly pour vegetable oil through feed tube into egg mixture. Process until all vegetable oil has been absorbed into egg and mixture thickens.

GREEN HERB MAYONNAISE

*Use this pretty green dressing with **Party Steamed Salmon**, page 51.*

1 recipe *Easy Mayonnaise*
3 tbs. minced fresh parsley

2 tbs. minced fresh dill
½ tsp. dried sweet basil, or 2 tbs. fresh

Make *Easy Mayonnaise*. Add fresh minced herbs to mayonnaise in food processor bowl and pulse 3 to 4 times to blend. Refrigerate until ready to serve.

STEAMED CHESTNUTS

Instead of heating chestnuts in a hot oven to make them easier to peel, try steaming them.

Cut a small cross in the flat side of each chestnut and steam in batches of 8 or 10 for 10 to 12 minutes, until hot. Remove from steamer and remove both outer shell and inner peel. Chestnuts peel easier when hot, so return them to steamer as they cool off and steam again for 2 to 3 minutes to soften shells.

After chestnuts are peeled, place them in a small bowl or plate and steam for about 30 minutes, until tender. Dice and add to your favorite stuffing or try them in *Chestnut and Celery Root Puree*, page 24.

NOTE: Instead using a steamer to soften shells, you can place a few chestnuts in a microwave-safe bowl with ½ cup water. Microwave on high for 2½ minutes. Peel when cool enough to handle.

CHESTNUT AND CELERY ROOT PUREE   Servings: 4-6

Chestnuts come on the market just in time to make this terrific accompaniment for the holiday bird. This can be made ahead and reheated.

1 lb. chestnuts, peeled (see page 23)
1 celery root, 8 oz.
2 tbs. butter
about ½ cup milk

2 tsp. lemon juice
salt and freshly ground pepper
minced parsley for garnish

Peel celery root by cutting off top and bottom. With a small sharp knife, cut down sides, removing rough peel. Cut out any brown bits that remain. Cut celery root into slices and then into ¾-inch cubes. Steam chestnuts and celery root for about 30 minutes until chestnuts are tender when pierced with a knife. Place chestnuts and celery root in the bowl of a food processor and pulse a few times. Add butter and about half the milk. Process until smooth, adding more milk if necessary. Season with salt, pepper and lemon juice. Sprinkle with parsley and serve hot.

VARIATIONS

- Use a small bulb of fresh fennel instead of the celery root.

- Steam a tart apple with the celery root and chestnuts.

SWEET CORN

Steaming is a wonderful way to cook sweet corn. You are only limited by the size of your steamer.

Remove corn husks and silk. Trim as needed. Spray steamer rack with non-stick cooking spray and place corn on rack. When steamer water comes to a boil, add corn to steamer and cook for about 10 minutes. Carefully remove corn from steamer and serve immediately.

LIME JALAPEÑO BUTTER

This zesty flavored butter is great on hot sweet corn.

4 tbs. softened butter
grated rind from 1 small lime
2 tsp. lime juice

1 small jalapeño pepper, seeded and
   minced, or to taste
salt and freshly ground pepper

Combine ingredients with softened butter. Pack into a small decorative bowl for serving immediately or form into a small log and roll up in waxed paper. Refrigerate and cut into slices to serve.

EGGPLANT SESAME DIP

Makes: 1¼ cups

Toasted sesame seeds, garlic and cumin give this dip a Middle Eastern flavor. Serve with crisp pita triangles or lavosh. The garlic cloves are steamed along with the eggplant and you don't have to peel them.

1 small eggplant, about 1 lb., stem
  removed, cut in half
5 whole garlic cloves
1 tbs. full-flavored olive oil
½ tsp. cumin
1 tbs. lemon juice
½ tsp. sesame oil

¼ tsp. salt
generous amount of freshly ground
  pepper
3-4 drops hot pepper sauce, optional
2 tbs. toasted sesame seeds
fresh cilantro leaves for garnish

Place eggplant, cut side down, with garlic cloves in steamer basket and steam for 20 to 25 minutes after water comes to a boil. Eggplant is cooked when a knife goes in easily. Remove from steamer. When eggplant is cool enough to handle, scoop out eggplant meat and discard skin. Place eggplant in a small bowl and mix well to break up pieces into a fairly smooth texture. Squeeze cooked garlic into eggplant, and add remaining ingredients except cilantro. Spoon into a serving bowl and garnish with cilantro leaves.

SPICY EGGPLANT APPETIZER

Makes 1½ cups

Serve with crisp pita chips or crackers. This can be made ahead and kept in the refrigerator for 2-3 days. It is based on a popular Chinese-style stir-fry. Steaming makes it a much lighter and less oily dish.

1 lb. eggplant
3-4 large cloves garlic, unpeeled
½ fresh red bell pepper
1 tbs. vegetable oil
3-4 green onions, thinly sliced
1 tsp. grated fresh ginger root

2 tsp. cider vinegar
1 tbs. soy sauce
¼ tsp. red pepper flakes or ¼ tsp.
   Chinese-style chili paste with garlic
½ tsp. sesame oil
fresh cilantro leaves for garnish

Cut stem from eggplant and cut in half lengthwise. Place cut sides down in a steamer basket and add fresh red pepper half and whole garlic cloves. Steam over high heat for 20 minutes until eggplant is done, or can be pierced easily with a knife blade. Allow to cool and remove skin. Coarsely chop steamed eggplant and pepper; squeeze garlic out of its skin. Heat oil in a large skillet and add eggplant, garlic, pepper, and remaining ingredients except sesame oil and cilantro leaves. Cook eggplant mixture over high heat until most of moisture evaporates. Remove from heat, stir in sesame oil, and place in a serving bowl. Garnish with cilantro leaves.

EGGPLANT WITH PLUM SAUCE

Servings: 4

Chinese-style plum sauce accents strips of eggplant and sautéed ground pork to make a flavorful side dish.

1/4 lb. ground pork
3/4 lb. small Japanese or Chinese eggplants, stems removed
1 large carrot, coarsely grated
3 green onions, thinly sliced
1 cup chicken stock
2 tbs. plum sauce
salt and white pepper

Cut unpeeled eggplant into 2x1/2-inch strips. Lightly brown ground pork in a medium nonstick skillet. Remove pork from skillet. Place eggplant and remaining ingredients in skillet. Bring to a boil and add browned pork. Pour eggplant mixture into a small heatproof bowl, cover with foil, place in steamer and steam covered for 35 to 40 minutes, until eggplant is tender. Serve immediately.

GARLIC

Whole garlic cloves steam beautifully. If your other vegetables are to steam for at least 20 minutes, toss in several garlic cloves and then squeeze the soft, sweet garlic puree over the vegetables. Or spread on bread, top with a little Parmesan cheese and toast for a few minutes in a hot oven.

FOR WHOLE HEADS OF GARLIC

Cut about ½-inch off the pointed end of the garlic head. Place on steamer rack and steam for 35 minutes, or until cloves are soft.

FOR INDIVIDUAL WHOLE CLOVES OF GARLIC

It is not necessary to peel the cloves. Steam for about 20 minutes, until cloves are soft.

SPINACH-STUFFED MUSHROOMS

Makes: 8

Large mushrooms are stuffed with a savory mixture of spinach, ricotta cheese and proscuitto. Serve hot, on small plates.

8 large mushrooms, 2-2½-inch diameter
4 tbs. butter
¼ cup finely chopped onion
2 cloves garlic, minced
½ cup chopped cooked spinach, squeezed very dry
½ cup ricotta cheese
¼ cup thinly sliced, diced proscuitto
¼ cup grated Parmesan cheese
1 tsp. dried sweet basil
dash nutmeg
salt and pepper

Prepare mushrooms by trimming off tip of stem; then twist out large stem piece. With a small spoon, scrape out some of the mushroom around the base of the stem to make a small cup. Chop stems and mushroom trimmings. Melt butter in a small skillet. Dip mushroom caps in butter, coating outside, and spoon a little butter into cup. Sprinkle with salt and pepper. Sauté onion and chopped mushroom in butter for 3 to 4 minutes until soft. Add garlic and spinach and continue to cook for another 2 to 3 minutes until spinach is quite dry. Remove from heat and let mixture cool for a few minutes. Add remaining ingredients to spinach mixture and mound stuffing in mushroom caps.

Bring water in steamer to a boil. Place mushrooms in steamer basket and lower into steamer. Cover and steam for 5 to 6 minutes, depending on size of mushrooms. Mushrooms are done when blade of a knife pierces side of mushroom easily. Remove from steamer basket with a large spoon and place on serving plates. Serve immediately.

STUFFED MUSHROOMS
WITH PEAS AND GRUYÈRE

Makes: 8

Use large 2- or 2½-inch mushrooms if you can find them. These make a great hot appetizer or first course served on small plates with forks.

8 large mushrooms
3 tbs. butter
salt and freshly ground pepper
¼ cup minced onion

¼ tsp. dried tarragon
½ cup small green peas, defrosted if frozen
½ cup grated Gruyère cheese

Prepare mushrooms as directed on page 30. Melt butter in a small skillet. Dip mushroom caps in butter, coating outside and spooning a little butter into cup. Sprinkle with salt and pepper. Sauté onion and mushroom pieces in butter for 3 to 4 minutes until soft. Stir in tarragon and green peas. Cook for 1 to 2 minutes. Remove from heat, allow to cool for a few minutes and then stir in grated cheese. Fill mushroom caps with stuffing mixture. Bring water in steamer to a boil. Place mushrooms in steamer basket and lower into steamer. Cover and steam for 5 to 6 minutes depending on size of mushrooms. Mushrooms are done when blade of a knife pierces side of mushroom easily.

GLAZED PEARL ONIONS

Tiny white or red boiling onions are a delicious accompaniment for roast chicken, baked ham or other meats. A quick 2 to 3 minutes of steaming makes them easier to peel.

1 pkg. (10 oz.) pearl onions,
  ½ - ¾-inch diameter
2 tbs. balsamic vinegar
1 tbs. butter

⅛ tsp. dried thyme
½ tsp. sugar
salt and freshly ground pepper

    Wash onions and place them unpeeled in one layer in steamer basket. Steam for 2 to 3 minutes after water comes to a boil. Carefully remove steamer basket and allow to stand until onions are cool enough to remove skins. Cut off stems, pull off skins, and cut a small cross on each stem end to help them stay together. Place peeled onions back in steamer basket and continue steaming for 5 to 6 minutes until a knife goes in easily.

    Heat remaining ingredients together in a small skillet. Add steamed onions to skillet and cook over medium heat 2 to 3 minutes until most liquid has evaporated and onions are lightly browned. These can be done ahead and gently reheated just before serving.

STEAMER POLENTA

Credit goes to Joyce Goldstein for her great technique of starting the traditional long-cooking polenta with cold water to avoid lumps and to Carlo Middione for the idea of steaming polenta to avoid the tedious 45 minutes of stirring while the polenta cooks. Polenta is a terrific basic recipe that can be served in many disguises. Combine it hot out of the pot with cheese and butter; pour it into a loaf pan or spread it in a large flat baking pan to cool, slice it, brush it with good olive oil or butter and grill it or bake it. Serve it hot with a fresh tomato or mushroom sauce, or fry it in butter for a hearty winter breakfast treat.

1 cup coarse cornmeal
2 cups cold water
1 tsp. salt

Combine corn meal, cold water and salt in a large saucepan. Bring to a boil over medium heat, add salt. Pour into a large heatproof bowl that will fit into the steamer basket. Cover bowl with foil and place on steamer rack. When steamer water boils steam for 45-50 minutes. Corn meal will have absorbed all water and will be soft and creamy at the end of the cooking time. If serving hot, season with additional salt, pepper and stir in some cheese or other flavorings. Polenta can be kept hot over steaming water for at least an hour before serving. Pour polenta into a 9x5-inch loaf pan or spread out in a jelly roll pan, allow to cool, and then cut into slices or other shapes. To grill, brush polenta slices with olive oil and place on a barbecue or run under a hot broiler until crisp and lightly brown.

POTATOES

Steaming is one of the best methods to use when cooking potatoes for a salad. The texture is firmer and they slice without crumbling. If using large potatoes, peel and cut the potatoes into the same size pieces so they cook in the same amount of time.

STEAMED NEW POTATOES

Place unpeeled, small new potatoes (1½ to 2 inches diameter) in a collapsible steamer basket or on steamer rack of steamer. Place potatoes in steamer and when steamer water comes to a boil, time potatoes for about 20 minutes. Cooking time will vary with number of potatoes in steamer. Test potatoes: if not completely cooked, replace cover and allow to steam for another few minutes. Serve hot with butter, salt and pepper; or allow to cool and use for a salad.

POTATO VEGETABLE COMBO

Steam several different vegetables together for a savory accompaniment to roast chicken or grilled meats. Put together your favorite combinations, but cut them in about the same size pieces so they will cook in the same amount of time.

1 tbs. full-flavored olive oil
3-4 small new potatoes, cut into quarters
2 small whole turnips, peeled, or cut larger turnip into pieces
4 pieces of carrot, each ¼-inch x 3 inches
4 red pepper strips, each ¼-inch x 3 inches
2 cloves garlic, peeled and cut in half
salt and freshly ground pepper
fresh or dried thyme
dash red pepper flakes

Toss vegetables with olive oil and seasonings in a small heatproof bowl that will fit into steamer with at least 1 inch of space for steam to circulate. Cover bowl tightly with foil and place on a rack in steamer. When steamer water boils, time vegetables to cook for about 30 minutes, or until vegetables test done with a knife. Carefully remove bowl from steamer and serve immediately.

SPAGHETTI SQUASH

Spaghetti squash is fun to cook. It steams very quickly — a 1½ lb. squash cooks in about 25 to 30 minutes. It is done when you can pierce it easily with a knife. Cut it in half lengthwise. Remove the seeds and deep gold stringy center with a fork and discard. Then pull the squash meat from the sides with a fork and you are rewarded with a light yellow mound of crisp tender squash strands. A 1½ lb. squash yields a little over 3 cups of "spaghetti."

SERVING SUGGESTIONS

- Sprinkle cooked squash with 2 tbs. melted butter, ½ cup grated Parmesan cheese and a dash of red pepper flakes and serve as a hot luncheon or side dish.

- Toss warm squash with *Arugula Pesto Sauce*, page 39, and serve as an entrée with hot garlic bread.

- Make *Squash Foo Yung*, page 40, or *Spaghetti Squash Frittata*, page 42.

- Treat it as a pasta and top with *Scallop and Red Pepper Sauce*, page 43, or *Spicy Peanut Sauce*, page 44.

ARUGULA PESTO

Makes: 1 cup

Spicy, peppery arugula makes a delicious substitute for fresh sweet basil in pesto. This keeps its bright green color. If you make it ahead, stir in about 1/3 cup of hot water so it mixes easily with spaghetti squash or cooked pasta.

1 cup arugula leaves, tightly packed
2 garlic cloves
1/2 cup pine nuts or blanched almonds
1/3 cup full-flavored olive oil
1/2 cup grated Parmesan cheese
1/2 tsp. salt
freshly ground pepper

Wash and dry arugula leaves, removing most stems. With the motor running, drop garlic into a food processor or blender and process until chopped. Add arugula and remaining ingredients and process until well blended, but not completely smooth. Refrigerate if not using immediately. This keeps well in the refrigerator for 3 to 4 days. Use as a sauce for cooked spaghetti squash or pasta, or as a topping for baked tomatoes.

SQUASH FOO YUNG

Steamed spaghetti squash is delectable in a classic Chinese-style egg foo yung. Serve it with a simple sauce of chicken stock, soy sauce and cornstarch. This is great for a late morning brunch or ski breakfast with a fruit cup.

2 medium dried Shiitaki mushrooms
2 cups cold cooked spaghetti squash
4 green onions, white part only, thinly sliced
3 eggs, lightly beaten
½ cup finely diced ham
generous grinds of black pepper
¼ cup vegetable oil

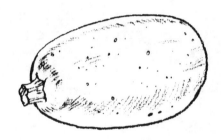

SAUCE
1 cup chicken stock
1 tbs. soy sauce
pinch of white pepper
1 tbs. cornstarch dissolved in 2 tbs. cold water

Soak Shiitaki mushrooms in hot water for 20 minutes to soften. Squeeze dry and cut out hard center stems. Cut into thin slivers. In a medium bowl, combine mushrooms, squash and green onions with beaten eggs. Stir in diced ham and pepper.

Make sauce by bringing chicken stock to a boil in a small saucepan. Add soy sauce and white pepper. Reduce heat and stir in dissolved cornstarch. Keep sauce warm while you are making foo yung.

Heat vegetable oil in a large nonstick skillet. When oil is simmering but not smoking, spoon egg mixture into oil, making six patties. Cook on one side until set but not brown, and then turn over, cooking about 3 minutes each side. Slide out onto paper towels to remove excess oil. Transfer to warm serving plates, spoon sauce over and serve immediately.

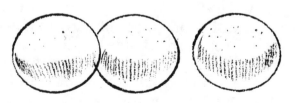

SPAGHETTI SQUASH FRITTATA

Servings: 2-3

A frittata makes great luncheon or picnic fare. The crisp yellow squash strands are accented with colorful red, yellow or green pepper slivers.

2 cups cold cooked spaghetti squash
4 eggs, lightly beaten
5 green onions, thinly sliced
1/3 cup thinly sliced yellow or green
  bell pepper
1/3 cup thinly sliced red bell pepper

1/3 cup grated Parmesan cheese
1 tsp. Dijon mustard
salt and freshly ground pepper
3 tbs. olive oil
4-5 medium mushrooms, thinly
  sliced

Combine squash with eggs, onions, peppers, cheese, mustard, salt and pepper. Heat 1 tbs. olive oil in a 7-or 8-inch skillet and sauté mushrooms 3 to 4 minutes until soft. Allow to cool for a few minutes and then add mushrooms to egg mixture. Wipe out skillet and add remaining 2 tablespoons of olive oil. When oil is hot, pour egg mixture into skillet. Cook over low heat until eggs begin to set. Lift around sides of pan so uncooked portion flows under cooked part. When partially set, place under broiler as far away from heat as possible for 5 to 10 minutes, until top is set and lightly browned. Slide out of pan onto a plate lined with paper towels. Let drain. Cut into wedges to serve warm or at room temperature.

SCALLOP AND RED PEPPER SAUCE FOR SPAGHETTI SQUASH

This quick sauce complements the crisp spaghetti squash strands. Serve with a green salad, garlic bread and a Pinot Grigio or Sauvignon Blanc.

2 tbs. butter
3 tbs. minced shallots
¾ cup heavy cream
½ cup diced roasted red peppers
  or pimiento

dash red pepper flakes
salt and freshly ground pepper
8 oz. bay scallops or larger scallops
  cut into ¾-inch pieces
3 cups cooked spaghetti squash

Melt butter in a medium skillet and sauté shallots 2 to 3 minutes over low heat until soft. Add cream, red peppers, red pepper flakes, salt and pepper. Bring cream to a boil and cook for 2 to 3 minutes over high heat until cream starts to thicken. Lower heat, add scallops and cook for another 2 to 3 minutes until scallops are just done. Do not overcook. Add spaghetti squash to skillet and toss with scallop mixture. Serve immediately in a warm bowl or on warmed plates.

SPICY PEANUT SAUCE

*This flavorful sauce combined with cooked spaghetti squash makes a hearty vegetarian entrée. Serve with sliced fresh pineapple or steamed **Gingered Orange Slices**, page 140.*

3/4 cup vegetable broth or chicken
  broth
1 tbs. minced fresh ginger root
1 tbs. minced fresh garlic
dash red pepper flakes
1/3 cup chunky peanut butter

2 tbs. soy sauce
1 tbs. sugar
2 tbs. rice wine vinegar
1 tsp. sesame oil
3 cups cooked spaghetti squash

In a small saucepan, bring vegetable broth to a boil and add fresh ginger, garlic and red pepper flakes. Simmer 2 to 3 minutes. Remove from heat and stir in peanut butter, soy sauce, sugar and rice wine vinegar. Mix well. Return to heat and cook over low heat 3 to 4 minutes until mixture is hot. Stir in sesame oil and toss with hot cooked spaghetti squash. Serve immediately.

STEAMED SPINACH

When steamed, spinach retains its bright green color and only needs a squeeze of lemon juice, butter and a little salt and pepper to make a delicious side dish.

Wash 1 lb. spinach well and remove long stems, if desired. Place spinach leaves in a colander or steamer basket that has been sprayed with nonstick cooking spray. When steamer water comes to a boil, add spinach to steamer and steam for about 5 to 6 minutes. If steaming more than one pound, increase cooking time. Do not overcook. Carefully remove from steamer, let cool slightly and gently press out excess liquid. Dress with lemon juice, butter, salt and pepper. Serve immediately.

STEAMED SWEET POTATOES OR YAMS

Chunks of steamed sweet potatoes or yams are delicious with a little butter, salt and pepper, or puree them for a creamy side dish.

Peel and cut potatoes into 1-inch cubes and place in a steamer basket that has been sprayed with nonstick cooking spray. When steamer water comes to a boil, carefully lower steamer basket into steamer and steam for 15 to 17 minutes. Test for doneness with a fork. Remove from steamer and serve immediately.

YAM OR SWEET POTATO AND APPLE MEDLEY

This is an appetizing light side dish for a holiday dinner or buffet. It is a perfect accompaniment for a baked ham or turkey, without being sticky sweet. The apples and yams are cut into slices about the same thickness and are assembled in rows in a 8x8-inch baking pan or other heatproof dish with sides that will fit into the steamer. Spoon any pan juices over the dish just before serving. This can be made ahead and reheated in the oven or in the microwave.

1 lb. yams or sweet potatoes
1 lb. tart green cooking apples
2 tbs. apple juice
2 tbs. maple syrup
¼ tsp. cinnamon
¼ tsp. ground cardamom
1 tbs. butter

Peel yams, cutting about 1/8-inch of peel from meat. Cut in half and then into 1/4-inch slices. Peel and core apples, cut into quarters and then into 1/4-inch slices so pieces are about the same size as yam slices. Combine apple juice, syrup, cinnamon and cardamom in a large bowl. Toss yam and apple slices in bowl with apple juice mixture. Spray a heatproof pan with nonstick spray. Standing slices on end, alternate rows of yam slices with rows of apple slices down length of pan. If you have extra apples, tuck in around sides. Pour apple juice mixture over yams and apples, and dot with tablespoon of butter.

When water comes to a boil, place pan on a steamer rack and cover steamer. Cook for about 25 minutes or until yams are tender. Remove from heat and allow to stand a few minutes. Tip pan and spoon juices over yams and apples just before serving.

ZUCCHINI-YELLOW SQUASH COMBO

Servings: 2

Combine some of your favorite vegetables and steam them together in a flavorful olive oil. Here is a savory squash, celery root and tomato medley.

1 small zucchini, stemmed and sliced
1 small yellow squash, stemmed and sliced
1 Roma tomato, coarsely chopped
⅓ cup diced celery root
1 large shallot, minced
1 tbs. olive oil
pinch of oregano
salt and pepper

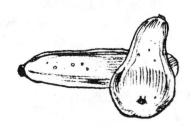

Toss vegetables with olive oil and seasonings. Place in a small heatproof bowl, cover with foil or a lid and place on a rack in steamer. When steamer water boils, time vegetables to steam about 20 minutes. Carefully remove bowl from steamer and serve immediately.

FISH AND SHELLFISH

Steaming is an excellent way to cook fish and shellfish. Lemon slices and juice, fresh tarragon, thyme or dill sprigs, green onion or lemon grass slivers, soy sauce, white wine, and rice wine or vinegar enhance the natural fish flavors. Steaming doesn't require the addition of fat or oil, resulting in tasty, lower calorie entrées. Just place the fish fillets on a small plate, top with lemon slices, your choice of herbs or wine, and steam either covered with plastic wrap or another slightly larger plate inverted over the fish. Steaming takes only 7 or 8 minutes, depending on size of the fish.

A quick rule of thumb in steaming fish is to cook it about 10 minutes per each inch of thickness at the thickest part. Allow the steamer water to come to a rolling boil before you start timing.

Included are some classic recipes for steaming shrimp, clams, mussels, crab and lobster. A wonderful *Salmon Salad Niçoise* is made with potatoes, beans and salmon, all done in the steamer. *Party Steamed Salmon* can be done in a large steamer, or improvise one with a roasting pan and some cans with both ends cut out to serve as a plate rack. *Seafood Terrine* is an elegant fish paté to be served as an impressive first course or for a buffet. Fresh trout are filled with a lemon and sweet basil bread crumb stuffing and steamed. Try the *Mexican-Style Fish Salad* for picnic or patio fare.

PARTY STEAMED SALMON

Servings: 4-6

Half of a salmon makes terrific buffet or party fare. If your steamer is very small you may want to improvise with a large roasting pan, wok or fish poacher. Make a support for the steamer plate with metal trivets or 7 oz. tuna fish or pineapple cans with the top and bottoms cut out to keep the steamer plate above the water. A good basic guide for steaming fish is 10 minutes per inch of thickness.

1 (3 lb.) section of fresh salmon,
  about 3 inches at the thickest

5-6 thin lemon slices
2-3 thin slices fresh ginger root

Wash fish and place 2 to 3 lemon slices and ginger root slices in fish cavity. Place remaining lemon slices on top of fish. Make sure your tray or plate will fit into the steamer basket with about 1 inch circulation space around it. Place fish on plate and put in steamer when water has come to a boil. Steam a 3 lb. fish about 20 to 25 minutes, or until internal temperature reaches 140°, and fish is firm to the touch. Remove from steamer, allow to cool for a few minutes and then peel off skin. Turn fish over and remove skin from the other side as well. Serve fish at room temperature or refrigerate if doing ahead. Serve with *Green Herb Mayonnaise*, page 22.

SALMON SALAD NIÇOISE

Servings: 3 to 4

This attractive salad is composed of fresh steamed vegetables and thin slices of salmon, accented with wedges of ripe tomatoes, egg slices, black olives and capers. Steam the vegetables first and allow to cool slightly before adding the dressing and arranging on a serving platter or individual salad plates. The salmon can be steamed just before serving or done ahead.

1 lb. tender green beans, stemmed, left whole
1 lb. red potatoes, peeled and cut into wedges or 1 lb. small new potatoes, unpeeled
2 hard boiled eggs
2 large ripe tomatoes, peeled, seeded, and cut into wedges
2 tbs. capers, drained and rinsed

15-20 black olives, preferably Kalamata or Niçoise
1 lb. salmon fillets, skinned and cut into 8 or 10 equal sized pieces
mixed salad greens or lettuce leaves
fresh chopped parsley or sweet basil leaves for garnish
Creamy Vinaigrette Dressing, follows

Steam beans 10 to 12 minutes and potatoes for 20 to 25 minutes, or until tender. Remove from steamer and refresh in cold water to stop cooking. Pat dry and drizzle with a little salad dressing. Steam salmon pieces 6 to 8 minutes, depending on size, until fish is firm to touch. Do not overcook. Remove from steamer and allow to cool slightly before arranging on salad.

To assemble: Coat mixed greens or lettuce leaves with a little dressing and place on a serving platter or individual salad plates. Arrange beans, potatoes and tomatoes around edge of platter. Place salmon pieces in the middle. Garnish with black olives and egg slices. Sprinkle with parsley and spoon more of the dressing over salad. Serve with French bread or bread sticks.

CREAMY VINAIGRETTE DRESSING

⅓ cup full-flavored olive oil
1 tbs. lemon juice
1 tbs. Dijon mustard
1 tbs. white wine vinegar

½ tsp. sugar
2-3 anchovies, rinsed, dried and
    finely chopped
salt and freshly ground pepper

Combine ingredients in a blender or food processor to form a creamy emulsion.

VARIATIONS

- Substitute fresh steamed ahi tuna or halibut for the salmon.

- Other colorful and delicious vegetables that could be used are red or yellow pepper rings, fresh steamed asparagus spears, cucumber slices, marinated artichoke hearts, or sliced pickled beets.

SHRIMP AND PEPPER KEBOBS

Servings: 2

Peeled shrimp are threaded on skewers with small pieces of red and yellow peppers placed between the shrimp. These are briefly steamed and then are brushed with a garlic butter sauce. Couscous mixed with a few green peas or chopped fresh tomato makes a delicious accompaniment. Serve with a crisp dry white wine.

16-20 medium sized shrimp, peeled and deveined
½ small red bell pepper, cut into 1-inch pieces

½ small yellow bell pepper, cut into 1-inch pieces

GARLIC BUTTER SAUCE
2 tbs. butter
2 small cloves garlic, minced
1 tsp. lemon juice

dash red pepper flakes
finely chopped parsley for garnish

Thread shrimp and pepper pieces on skewers, 4 to 5 shrimp per skewer, alternating shrimp and pepper pieces. Make garlic butter sauce by melting butter in a small saucepan and cooking garlic in butter for 1 to 2 minutes. Do not allow garlic to brown. Add lemon juice and red pepper flakes.

Place skewers in steamer basket. When water comes to a boil, lower steamer basket into steamer and steam for 2 to 3 minutes, until shrimp turn pink. Do not overcook. Remove from steamer, brush with garlic butter and sprinkle with parsley. If serving over couscous, spoon hot couscous on plate, top with shrimp skewers and drizzle with garlic butter sauce.

COUSCOUS

3/4 cup water or vegetable stock
1 tbs. butter
1/2 cup quick cooking couscous

1/3 cup small green peas, defrosted if frozen or 1 small tomato, peeled, seeded, chopped

Bring water and butter to boil in a small saucepan or skillet. Add couscous and peas, stir, cover and remove from heat. Let stand 5 minutes and then fluff with a fork. If using chopped tomato, stir in just before serving. Serve immediately.

VARIATIONS

- Instead of the peppers, place Chinese pea pods or pieces of red onion between the shrimp. Serve with *Lime Jalapeño Butter*, page 25.

- Large scallops or 1½-inch pieces of halibut or salmon can be used with or instead of the shrimp. Make sure the pieces of fish and shrimp or scallops are about the same size so they cook in the same amount of time.

SOLE STUFFED WITH SHRIMP

Servings: 2

These easy and elegant sole rolls stuffed with shrimp make a light entrée or first course, and can be served hot or cold. If using as an appetizer, either buy the smallest sole fillets you can find or split large pieces. Increase this recipe for the desired number of servings.

2 fillets of sole, 4-5 oz. each
2 oz. salad shrimp
salt and freshly ground pepper
4 thin lemon slices

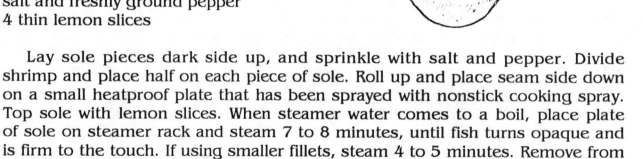

Lay sole pieces dark side up, and sprinkle with salt and pepper. Divide shrimp and place half on each piece of sole. Roll up and place seam side down on a small heatproof plate that has been sprayed with nonstick cooking spray. Top sole with lemon slices. When steamer water comes to a boil, place plate of sole on steamer rack and steam 7 to 8 minutes, until fish turns opaque and is firm to the touch. If using smaller fillets, steam 4 to 5 minutes. Remove from steamer and serve hot with *Tarragon Sauce* or allow to cool, refrigerate and serve chilled with *Green Herb Mayonnaise*, page 22.

TARRAGON SAUCE

2½ tbs. butter
2 tbs. flour
8 oz. bottled clam juice
¼ tsp. tarragon
salt and pepper
2 tbs. heavy cream

Melt butter in a small saucepan, add flour and cook 2 minutes, stirring constantly. Gradually add clam juice and cook until sauce thickens. Stir in tarragon, salt, pepper and heavy cream. Spoon over sole rolls.

MEXICAN-STYLE FISH SALAD

Servings: 4-5

This salad has the fresh flavors of a seviche, with steamed fish marinated in a lemon and lime juice dressing and garnished with avocado, tomato and fresh cilantro. This is a wonderful warm day luncheon salad or picnic fare.

1 lb. sea bass or other firm-fleshed fish
½ jalapeño pepper, stem and seeds removed
1 tbs. light olive oil
1 tbs. lemon juice
1 tbs. lime juice
½ fresh jalapeño pepper, seeds removed, finely minced
2 green onions, finely chopped
¼ tsp. oregano
salt and pepper
½ tsp. hot pepper sauce or Tabasco Sauce
1 avocado, peeled and diced
1 fresh tomato, peeled, seeded and diced
2 tbs. roasted red pepper, finely chopped
fresh cilantro for garnish

Place fish and jalapeño pepper half on a plate. Place in steamer and steam for about 10 to 15 minutes, depending on thickness of fish. Fish is done when firm to touch or at 130°. Remove from steamer and allow to cool. Cut fish into ¾-inch pieces and toss with olive oil, lemon and lime juice, diced cooked jalapeño and fresh jalapeño, onions, oregano, salt, pepper and hot sauce. Refrigerate for at least an hour before serving.

Add avocado, tomato and red pepper pieces just before serving. Garnish with fresh cilantro leaves. Spoon into lettuce cups for individual servings or serve on a platter, garnished with lemon slices and more cilantro.

HOMEMADE TARTAR SAUCE

Makes: 1 cup

This is a pretty piquant sauce to serve with steamed salmon, shrimp and other seafood.

1 large egg
1 tsp. lemon juice
1 tsp. white wine vinegar
1 tsp. Dijon mustard
salt and white pepper
dash hot pepper sauce

¾ cup vegetable oil
3 tbs. minced fresh parsley
2 tbs. finely chopped fresh dill
2 green onions, finely chopped
2 tbs. finely chopped dill pickle
2 tsp. capers, drained and chopped

Place egg, lemon juice, vinegar, mustard, salt, pepper and pepper sauce in the bowl of a food processor and process for a few seconds to blend. With motor running, gradually add vegetable oil and process until mixture thickens. Add remaining ingredients and pulse 3 or 4 times to combine. Refrigerate until ready to serve.

STEAMED BLUE CRABS, MARYLAND STYLE

Atlantic blue crabs have the sweetest, tenderest and juiciest meat of any crab. For a great informal party you need only the cooked crabs, crusty bread and beer. Spread newspapers on the table and pile the crabs in the middle. Give each person a steak knife with a solid handle which can be used to both crack the shells and pick the meat. Be sure to put a roll of paper towels on the table. After the meal, just roll everything up in the newspapers and discard.

10-12 live Atlantic blue crabs per
  person
3 tbs. Old Bay seasoning

3 tbs. sea salt
white vinegar
water

Add enough water and vinegar in equal amounts to an enamel or stainless steel pot to cover bottom to a depth of 2 inches. Cover pot and bring to a rapid boil. Put live crabs in a basket or container that can be suspended over boiling liquid. Sprinkle crabs with crab seasoning and salt. Put basket in pot and immediately replace the cover. Steam crabs for 20 minutes. Allow crabs to cool. They can be eaten immediately, or kept for 2 days in the refrigerator. Use the meat in crab soup, salad or to make wonderful crab cakes.

STEAMED DUNGENESS CRAB

The Dungeness crab is found off the west coast from central California to Alaska. The meat is not as delicate or sweet as that of the blue crab, but it comes in much larger pieces, and the crabs are much easier to clean. Steaming over plain water is the perfect way to cook Dungeness crab. To steam, cover a large kettle with 1-2 inches of water in the bottom and bring to a rapid boil. Remove cover and place live crab on a rack on its back. Steaming time depends on the size of the crab. A 1½ pound crab should be steamed for 18 minutes, a 2-2½ pounder for 20 minutes, and over 3 pounds for 22 minutes. Plunge cooked crab into cold water and either clean immediately, or refrigerate for up to 3 days and clean just before serving.

To clean, lay cooked crab on its back, and lift and remove the triangular tail flap. Insert a thumb between shell and body, and lift body away from shell. Scoop out soft material between body sections, and remove gray gills or "dead man's fingers" from above legs. Wash well under running water. The crab is now ready to crack and eat. To crack, remove legs, place a thin edge on a solid surface, and tap with a mallet to crack the shell. Separate the two sections of body meat. The crab is now ready to serve. Serve with crusty sourdough bread, mayonnaise or *European-Style Seafood Cocktail Sauce*, page 63, and a crisp chardonnay.

EUROPEAN-STYLE SEAFOOD COCKTAIL SAUCE

This is a delicate mayonnaise-based sauce for shrimp, crab and fish salads.

1 cup good quality mayonnaise,
  preferably homemade
1 tbs. cognac
1 tbs. tomato paste

1 tbs. lemon juice
1 tsp. prepared horseradish
pinch of white pepper

Whisk ingredients together and refrigerate until ready to serve.

MARINATED DUNGENESS CRAB

Another simple delicious way to serve fresh crab is to marinate it in your favorite Italian-style salad dressing. Serve it to good friends with lots of napkins.

1 crab, cleaned and cracked

⅓ cup Italian-style salad dressing

Place cracked crab pieces in a large stainless, glass or plastic bowl. Pour salad dressing over crab, turning to coat all pieces. Cover and refrigerate for 3 to 4 hours or overnight. Remove from refrigerator about 30 minutes before serving. Pour any dressing remaining in dish into small bowls and serve for dipping crabmeat or bread.

CRABMEAT QUESADILLAS

This is a great appetizer or serve with a green salad for lunch.

FOR EACH QUESADILLA

1 tbs. cream cheese
1 tbs. grated Monterey Jack cheese
1 tsp. grated Parmesan cheese
1-2 tsp. prepared salsa
 crabmeat, cooked and flaked

fresh cilantro leaves
1 tsp. butter
2 fresh flour tortillas, about 8-inch
 diameter

Spread tortilla with cream cheese. Sprinkle with Monterey and Parmesan cheeses. Top with salsa, crabmeat and fresh cilantro leaves. Press second tortilla down firmly over the filling. Melt butter in a nonstick skillet and slide filled tortilla into pan. Cook over medium heat until tortilla is lightly browned and cheese starts to melt. With a wide spatula, turn tortilla over and brown other side. Slide out onto a cutting board and cut into 6 to 8 pieces. Serve immediately.

VARIATION

- Combine cream cheese with ½ tsp. prepared horseradish. Spread over tortilla, top with chopped pimiento or roasted red peppers, cheeses, crabmeat and chopped Italian parsley.

STEAMED MUSSELS

Steamed mussels are delicious when simply steamed and eaten with some of the broth. Serve with lots of hot bread and a crisp white wine.

2 lbs. mussels
6-8 lemon slices
2 shallots, finely chopped
1 bay leaf
red pepper flakes

2-3 sprigs parsley
1 sprig of fresh thyme, or pinch of
  dried
⅓ cup dry white wine or vermouth
1½ cups water

Scrub mussels with a small brush and pull off "beards." Wash shells under cold running water, rubbing shells together. Squeeze each shell and if it does not close tightly, discard it. In a pot large enough to hold all mussels, add all ingredients except mussels. Cover, bring to a boil and simmer for 3 to 4 minutes. Add cleaned mussels, cover and steam over high heat for 5 to 6 minutes until all mussels have opened. Remove mussels from pot, place in shallow soup plates, and strain broth over mussels. Serve immediately.

SEA BASS WITH ORANGE AND BLACK BEAN SAUCE

This preparation is also great with any firm-fleshed fish such as halibut, salmon, snapper. The fish is quickly steamed and the aromatic orange and black bean sauce is poured over it. Serve with hot steamed rice.

1 lb. piece of sea bass
3/4 cup orange juice
2 green onions, cut into slivers
grated rind of 1 orange
1 tbs. vegetable oil
1 tbs. fermented black beans, rinsed, drained and minced
2 cloves garlic, minced
1 tbs. minced ginger root
2 tbs. soy sauce
1 tsp. cornstarch
1/2 tsp. sesame oil

Place sea bass in a shallow dish that will fit into steamer basket with about an inch clearance for steam circulation. Add 2 tbs. of orange juice and top with slivered onion pieces. When steamer water boils, place fish on a steamer rack, cover steamer and steam for about 6 minutes, or until fish feels springy to touch. Carefully remove from steamer and set aside.

While fish is steaming, heat oil in a small skillet and sauté black beans, garlic, ginger and orange rind for 1 to 2 minutes to bring out flavor. Dissolve cornstarch in remaining orange juice and add to skillet with soy sauce. Pour juices from steamed fish into pan. Bring sauce to a boil and cook 1 to 2 minutes until sauce thickens. Pour over steamed fish and serve hot.

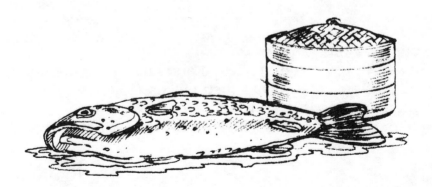

SEAFOOD TERRINE

Makes: 12-14 slices

This is an elegant fish paté with strips of green spinach, pink salmon and chunks of shrimp and scallop running through it. Make ahead and refrigerate several hours or overnight before serving as a first course or part of a buffet table.

1 lb. boneless firm fleshed fish, such as snapper, sea bass, halibut
1 egg
3 egg whites
1 cup heavy cream
2 tsp. prepared horseradish
2 tbs. lemon juice
½ tsp. salt
generous amount of white pepper
¼ lb. uncooked shrimp, peeled, deveined and cut into ½-inch pieces
¼ lb. uncooked scallops, cut into ½-inch pieces
4 oz. fresh salmon, cut into thin strips
15 or 20 large spinach leaves, blanched and dried on paper towels

Cut fish into 2-inch chunks and place in the bowl of a food processor. Pulse 10 to 12 times to break up fish. Add egg, egg whites, cream, horseradish, lemon juice, salt and pepper. Process until mixture is quite smooth. Fold shrimp and scallops into mixture. Oil a 9x5-inch loaf pan or other heatproof dish that will fit into steamer. Place a strip of parchment or waxed paper in bottom of pan for easy unmolding. Spread ⅓ of fish mixture into bottom of pan. Top with half of salmon strips and place half of spinach leaves between salmon strips. Top with another ⅓ of fish mixture and repeat salmon and spinach layer. Finish with remaining fish mixture.

Cover pan tightly with foil and place on a steamer rack. When steamer water comes to a boil, place rack in steamer and steam for 1 hour, or until mixture is firm and an inserted knife blade comes out clean. Allow to cool in pan for 20 minutes and then unmold on a plate. If there is extra liquid from fish on plate, pour off or use paper towels to absorb it. Allow to cool completely, cover and refrigerate until ready to serve.

This is easier to slice after it has chilled for several hours. Spoon some *Red Pepper Cream Sauce*, page 70, over each slice, or top with a dollop of *Green Herb Mayonnaise*, page 22.

RED PEPPER CREAM SAUCE

Makes: 1 cup

3 tbs. roasted red pepper, pureed in food processor or blender
1 tbs. lemon juice
1/4 tsp. Tabasco Sauce or to taste
1/2 cup heavy cream, whipped until soft peaks form
salt and white pepper

Combine pepper puree, lemon juice and hot sauce and fold into whipped cream. Serve immediately.

RED PEPPER YOGURT SAUCE

Makes: 3/4 cup

3 tbs. roasted red pepper, pureed in food processor or blender
1/4 tsp. Tabasco Sauce or to taste
1/2 cup low fat yogurt
1/4 tsp. sugar
salt and white pepper

Mix ingredients until well blended. Refrigerate until ready to serve.

STEAMED CLAMS

Steaming is the classic way to prepare clams. Plan to soak the clams for an hour to get rid of the sand before you cook them. These are a delicious low calorie appetizer or part of a light supper.

2 lb. fresh clams in shell
1 tbs. kosher or sea salt
water to cover
½ cup white wine

1 shallot, peeled and coarsely
   chopped
red pepper flakes

Scrub clams with a small brush and place in a bowl with water to cover. Add salt and allow to stand for an hour, stirring clams around once or twice. Rinse clams and place in a shallow bowl with sides that will fit into steamer with an inch clearance for steam to circulate. Add white wine, shallot and red pepper flakes. When steamer water comes to a boil, time clams to steam for 15 to 18 minutes or until shells open. Discard any clams that do not open. Remove clams from steamer and serve in individual bowls. Strain wine and shallot liquid through a filter or cheesecloth and pour over clams. Serve with hot garlic bread and a crisp white wine.

STUFFED CLAM APPETIZERS

Servings: 3-4

After you have steamed clams, top them with a savory bread crumb topping and bake them.

16-18 clams, steamed in their shells
2 tbs. butter
3 green onions, white part only, finely chopped
2 cloves garlic, minced
1/4 tsp. oregano
1/2 cup fresh bread crumbs
2 tbs. chopped parsley

With a small knife, loosen clam from bottom of clam shell but leave clam in shell. Remove other half of clam shell and discard. Melt butter in a small skillet and sauté onions and garlic for 2 to 3 minutes until soft. Add oregano and fresh bread crumbs. Mix well so bread crumbs absorb butter in skillet. Top each clam with bread crumb mixture. Bake in a 400° oven for about 10 minutes until clams are hot and bread crumbs are lightly browned. Sprinkle with parsley and serve immediately.

STUFFED TROUT

Fresh trout are stuffed with a fresh lemony bread crumb filling and steamed. You may have to remove the head and bend the tail a little so they fit on the steamer plate. Ask to have the trout scaled and boned when you buy them. A general guide for cooking fish is about 10 minutes per inch of thickness.

1 (12 oz.) or 2 (5-6 oz.) boned trout
2 tbs. butter
2 green onions, thinly sliced
¼ tsp. dried sweet basil or 2 tsp.
  fresh chopped basil

zest from 1 lemon
½ cup fresh bread crumbs
1 tbs. chopped parsley
salt and freshly ground pepper
lemon slices

Sauté onions in butter for 2 to 3 minutes until soft. Add sweet basil, lemon zest, fresh bread crumbs and parsley. Mix until bread crumbs have absorbed butter. Season inside of trout with salt and pepper and spoon in stuffing. Pull edges together, securing with one or two skewers to hold stuffing inside trout. Spray a small plate that will fit into steamer with nonstick spray. Place trout on plate and cover with thin slices of lemon. When steamer water boils, place trout in steamer and cover steamer. Steam for about 20 minutes for 1 large trout. Two smaller trout should be checked at 12 to 15 minutes.

SALMON-STUFFED GRAPE LEAVES

Makes: 20-22

These are a delicious accompaniment for champagne or serve them as part of an appetizer or salad platter.

2 tbs. olive oil
¼ cup minced onion
¼ cup minced celery hearts
8 oz. fresh salmon, finely chopped
⅔ cup cooked rice
2 tbs. fresh minced dill, or 2 tsp. dried dill weed
salt and freshly ground pepper
2 tbs. lemon juice
22-25 grape leaves
1¼ cups water

Sauté onion and celery in olive oil for 5 to 6 minutes over very low heat until vegetables are tender but not brown. Allow to cool before adding to salmon. Remove skin from salmon and chop finely. Combine salmon with rice, dill, salt, pepper, 1 tbs. lemon juice and onion mixture.

Rinse grape leaves under running water. Separate and trim off long stems with scissors. Place grape leaves shiny side down on a plate or board. Place a heaping teaspoon of filling at stem end of leaf, and roll up jelly roll fashion, tucking in sides of leaves as you roll. If grape leaves are quite large, trim sides to make a smaller leaf. Line a 9-inch round pan or one that fits into steamer with 1 or 2 grape leaves. Place filled grape leaves on top and sprinkle with lemon juice. Top with an extra grape leaf or trimmings and pour in water. Place a small heatproof plate over rolls to hold them down in liquid. Place on a steamer rack. After steamer water boils, steam rolls for 40 minutes. Remove pan from steamer and allow to stand about 10 minutes. Remove rolls to a plate and let cool. Serve warm or at room temperature.

These can be made ahead and refrigerated. Remove from refrigerator about 30 minutes before serving.

STEAMED LOBSTER

Steaming is a classic way to prepare lobster. Serve with nut or crab crackers.

Place about 2 to 3 inches of water in bottom of steamer and bring to a boil. Place lobster on a steamer rack above water, cover steamer and steam 10 to 12 minutes for a 1 lb. lobster. Steam a 1¼ lb. lobster 12 to 15 minutes. Remove from steamer and allow to cool enough to handle. Turn lobster on its back and cut it lengthwise deep enough to clean it but not completely through shell. Clean lobster under running water. Serve immediately with hot melted butter, or paint with garlic butter and run under broiler for 3 to 4 minutes to heat through.

GARLIC BUTTER (for 2 lobsters)
4 tbs. butter
2 large garlic cloves, minced

1 tbs. dry sherry
salt and pepper

Combine butter and minced garlic in a small microwavable dish and cook on high 45 seconds, until butter is melted. Add sherry, salt and pepper. Brush inside of lobsters with butter mixture and place under broiler for 3 to 4 minutes. Serve remaining garlic butter with lobsters.

POULTRY

The steaming process produces wonderfully moist and flavorful chicken, turkey and duck with little fat. Turkey breasts, stuffed or unstuffed, steam in less time than when cooked in the oven. Try *Turkey Breast Stuffed with Goat Cheese and Peppers*, or with *Spinach and Ricotta* for an elegant entrée. Whole chickens are delicious when steamed with some aromatics and make wonderful salads or sandwiches. Steaming has to be the best way to cook a duck because you have flavorful, juicy meat and the fat has been steamed out. If you have any leftover duck, make a *Duck Quesadilla* or *Duck and Lentil Salad*.

One way to add a little color to steamed poultry is to brush it lightly with mustard before steaming, or soy sauce after steaming, if you aren't serving a sauce. For whole steamed duck, paint the duck breast with soy, hoisin or plum sauce and heat it in a hot oven for a few minutes to crisp the skin and brown it.

For recipes with longer steaming times, be sure to check the level of the water in the steamer every 20 to 30 minutes and add more water when necessary so the steamer doesn't run dry.

WHOLE STEAMED TURKEY BREAST
Servings: 6-8

Frozen rolled turkey breasts actually steam faster than they roast in the oven and are moist and tender. A 4 lb. breast steams in just under 2 hours, depending on starting temperature and how thoroughly it has been defrosted. Serve with the packaged gravy pack or make your own sauce. Leftovers make great savory sandwiches for the lunch box.

4 lb. rolled turkey breast, defrosted and unwrapped (leave interior
  string netting on roast to steam)

Spray a small plate that will fit into steamer with about 1-inch clearance for steam to circulate. Place roast on plate and place in steamer. When water comes to a boil, cover and steam for 1¾ to 2 hours or until internal temperature is 160°. Remove from steamer and allow to stand for 10 to 15 minutes before slicing and serving hot, or cool before covering and refrigerating.

STEAMED WHOLE CHICKEN
WITH FRESH SAGE AND LEMON

This cooking method results in wonderfully moist chicken. Thin lemon slices and fresh sage leaves are placed under the skin for a fragrant accent. Remove the chicken from the refrigerator about an hour before steaming for faster cooking.

1 whole chicken, about 3½ lb.
4-5 thin lemon slices, seeds removed
6-8 fresh sage leaves
additional sage leaves, stems and pieces of lemon for stuffing chicken
2 cloves garlic, smashed
generous amount of water for steamer

Prepare chicken by removing giblets, washing and drying. Carefully slip your fingers between skin and breast meat to loosen skin. Continue loosening skin down to thighs. Put thin slices of lemon and sage leaves under skin to flavor meat. Add a few sage leaves and stems, pieces of lemon and garlic cloves to cavity. Truss chicken and place on a plate on steaming rack in steamer. Cover steamer and bring water to a boil. Steam a 3½ lb. chicken for about 1 hour and 15 minutes after water is steaming. Check steamer every 20 to 30 minutes to make sure there is enough water. If water is low, add about 2 cups boiling water to pot to continue steaming. Remove chicken from steamer and allow to set up for 10 to 15 minutes before carving. Serve warm or refrigerate and use for salads and sandwiches.

NOTE: A 3 lb. chicken will steam in about 1 hour; a 4 lb. chicken will take about 1½ to 1¾ hours to steam.

TURKEY BREAST STUFFED WITH SPINACH AND RICOTTA

Servings: 4-5

The bright green spinach makes an attractive center accent when the turkey breast is sliced and served. The turkey cooks much faster in the steamer than when oven-roasted.

1 half turkey breast (1-1¾ lbs.),
  boned, skin removed and reserved
3 thin slices prosciutto
1 tbs. olive oil
½ cup finely chopped onion

½ pkg. frozen chopped spinach,
  defrosted and squeezed very dry
⅔ cup ricotta cheese
¼ cup grated Parmesan cheese
salt, freshly ground pepper, and dash
  of nutmeg

Starting with thick side of turkey breast and using a long sharp knife, make a horizontal cut through center of meat, stopping about 2 inches from thin edge of breast. Open up breast like a book. Make several diagonal slashes in thicker portions of meat about ½-inch deep to relax meat. Reserve turkey skin to drape over top while steaming.

Place prosciutto slices over turkey meat. Melt oil in a small skillet and sauté onion 4 to 5 minutes until softened. Add well-drained spinach and cook another 2 to 3 minutes. Allow to cool slightly and stir in cheeses, salt, pepper and nutmeg. Arrange stuffing down center of flattened turkey breast over prosciutto. Pull up sides and hold in place with 2 or 3 skewers while you tie the roll at 1½-inch to 2-inch intervals. If turkey meat does not completely cover stuffing on the ends, place a small piece of foil under string to hold in stuffing.

Place turkey roll on a small deep plate that will fit into steamer, leaving at least 1 inch around it for steam circulation. Drape reserved skin over turkey roll. When water boils, place steamer basket in steamer, cover, and steam turkey about 35 to 45 minutes. Check with a meat thermometer at 35 minutes; continue to cook until internal temperature reaches 160°. Remove turkey from steamer and allow to set up 10 to 15 minutes before slicing. Cut into ¼-inch slices. Serve warm with *Wine Butter Sauce* or serve cold with a thin mayonnaise.

WINE BUTTER SAUCE

3 tbs. butter
2 tbs. flour
3 green onions or shallots, thinly sliced
1 cup chicken stock

½ cup dry white wine
1 tsp. prepared Dijon mustard, or
 ¼ tsp. dried
salt and white pepper

Melt butter in a small saucepan. Stir in flour and cook 2 to 3 minutes. Add onions and cook for another minute. Gradually stir in chicken stock and wine and bring to a boil. Add mustard, salt and pepper. Cook until sauce thickens.

TURKEY BREAST STUFFED WITH GOAT CHEESE AND PEPPERS

Servings: 4-5

A savory stuffing of roasted red and yellow peppers, black olives and goat cheese makes an attractive and delicious entrée for a summer dinner or a special party. Serve hot with **Wine Butter Sauce**, *page 83, or cold with* **Red Pepper Yogurt Sauce**, *page 70.*

1 boned turkey breast, 1½-1¾ lbs.
1 tsp. butter
1 tbs. chopped shallots
1 clove garlic, minced
4 oz. creamy goat cheese
1 egg
¼ tsp. thyme
⅓ cup diced roasted red or/and yellow peppers
4 Kalamata olives, pitted and coarsely chopped
1 tbs. grated Parmesan cheese

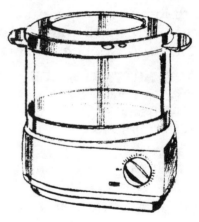

Starting with thick side of turkey breast and using a long sharp knife, make a horizontal cut through center of meat, stopping about 2 inches from thin edge of breast. Open up breast like a book. Make several diagonal slashes in thicker portions of meat about ½-inch deep to relax meat. Reserve turkey skin to drape over top while steaming.

Sauté shallots and garlic in butter for 1 to 2 minutes to soften. Let cool slightly and combine with remaining ingredients. Salt and pepper turkey breast and spread filling down middle of meat. Pull up sides and hold in place with 2 or 3 skewers while you tie roll at 1½-inch to 2-inch intervals. If turkey meat does not completely cover stuffing on ends, place a small piece of foil under string to hold in stuffing while it steams. Place turkey roll on a small deep plate that will fit into steamer, leaving at least 1 inch around it for steam circulation. Drape reserved skin over turkey roll.

When water boils, place steamer basket in steamer, cover, and steam turkey about 35 to 45 minutes. Check with a meat thermometer at 35 minutes and continue to cook until internal temperature reaches 160°. Remove turkey from steamer and allow to set up 10 to 15 minutes before serving warm, or allow to cool and refrigerate until ready to serve.

CONFETTI TURKEY TERRINE

Makes: 16 slices

Grated apple gives this terrine a light, moist texture. For a new look, substitute diced red peppers, black olives and green beans, or another colorful vegetable combination. Serve with a dollop of mayonnaise and some crusty rolls. This makes an attractive luncheon or buffet dish — or take it on a picnic.

⅓ cup chopped onion
1 small clove garlic, minced
2 tbs. vegetable oil
1 lb. ground turkey meat
1 medium tart apple, peeled, coarsely grated
1 large carrot, peeled, coarsely grated
1 tbs. Worcestershire sauce
1 tbs. Dijon mustard
¼ tsp. dried tarragon or sweet basil
1 egg, beaten
salt and freshly ground pepper
⅓ cup frozen peas

Sauté onion and garlic in oil for 4 to 5 minutes over low heat until onion softens. Let cool before adding to turkey mixture. Combine turkey and onion in a large mixing bowl with remaining ingredients, stirring in peas last. Spray a 4- to 5-cup loaf pan or baking mold with nonstick spray. Fill pan with meat mixture. When water in steamer comes to a boil, place pan in steamer basket and place in steamer. Wrap inside of steamer lid with a dish towel or lay a piece of foil over mold so moisture does not drip down onto meat.

Steam for 35 to 40 minutes. Check with a meat thermometer at 35 minutes and continue to steam for a few more minutes until an internal temperature of 170° is reached. Carefully remove pan from steamer and pour off accumulated liquid. Scrape off coagulated meat juices for a more attractive appearance. Cover meat with a small piece of aluminum foil and weight down with a heavy can until cool. Refrigerate for several hours before serving. Cut into 1/2-inch to 3/4-inch slices to serve.

PERFECT STEAMED DUCK

Steaming is one of the best ways to cook duck. Most of the fat is cooked out and the meat is wonderfully moist and tender. After steaming, coat the duck skin with honey and soy sauce, and roast in a hot oven for about 20 minutes to crisp the skin. If preparing duck for a dinner party, the duck can be steamed and then sauced and reheated in the oven just before serving.

1 duck, 4-4½ lbs.
4 green onions, including green tops
2 large cloves garlic
2 quarter-sized slices fresh ginger root
1 tsp. soy sauce
1 tbs. honey

The duck will release a large amount of fat and moisture during steaming. If your steamer has a shallow reservoir, place duck in a deep-sided heatproof dish to collect juices. Place onions, garlic and ginger inside duck. Use a small plate that fits into steamer with about 1-inch clearance for steam to circulate. Spray with nonstick spray and place duck on plate in steamer. Cut duck into quarters if necessary to fit into steamer. Place a generous amount of water in the steamer, bring it to a boil and steam duck for about 1½ hours until it reaches 180°. Check water level in steamer, adding more when necessary.

Preheat oven to 450°. Remove duck from steamer. Heat soy sauce and honey together so they will spread easily, and brush over duck skin. Roast for 20 to 25 minutes in hot oven until skin is brown and crisp. Cut into serving pieces and serve immediately.

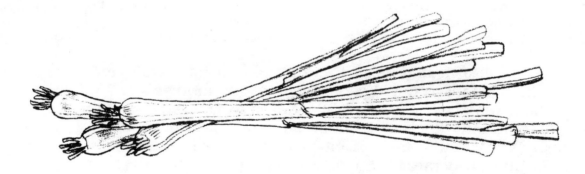

DUCK AND LENTIL SALAD

Servings: 4

Any leftover steamed duck can be added to cooked lentils for a terrific picnic or luncheon salad.

3 tbs. full-flavored olive oil
½ cup finely chopped onions
½ cup finely diced carrots
½ cup finely chopped celery
1 large garlic clove, minced
2 tbs. sherry or white wine vinegar

salt and freshly ground pepper
1½ cups cooked duck, cut into
  ¾-inch pieces
1 cup cooked small French green
  lentils
¼ cup chopped fresh cilantro leaves

Heat oil in a medium skillet and sauté onions, carrots and celery pieces 6 to 7 minutes until soft. Add garlic and cook for another 1 to 2 minutes. Remove from heat and allow to cool slightly. Stir in wine vinegar, salt and pepper. Toss to combine. Add duck and lentils, adding a little more olive oil if not moist enough. Garnish with fresh cilantro. This salad can be made ahead and keeps well in the refrigerator for 1 or 2 days. Remove from refrigerator 20 to 30 minutes before serving. Garnish with cilantro leaves just before serving.

DUCK QUESADILLA

Make this delicious quick appetizer when you have leftover steamed duck.

FOR EACH SERVING

2 fresh flour tortillas
1-2 tsp. hoisin sauce
1/4 cup shredded mozzarella cheese
several thin slices or slivers of
   cooked duck meat

1 green onion, white part only, cut
   into long thin slivers
fresh cilantro leaves from 5 or 6 stems
1 tsp. butter

Spread both flour tortillas very lightly on one side with hoisin sauce. Distribute mozzarella cheese over one tortilla, and then add slivers of duck meat. Sprinkle with onion and cilantro leaves. Place second tortilla sauce-side down on top of first tortilla. Press tortillas firmly together. Melt butter in a medium nonstick skillet just large enough to hold tortilla. Place filled tortilla in skillet and heat over low heat 2 to 3 minutes, until bottom is lightly browned. Carefully turn tortilla over and cook other side 2 to 3 minutes. Slide out on a cutting board and cut into wedges before serving.

NOTE: Also see *Steamed Duck Buns*, page 130.

PEKING-STYLE CHICKEN THIGHS

Makes: 6

Chicken thighs are steamed in a hoisin-flavored sauce. Serve with hot rice or noodles to soak up the sauce. If there are any pieces left over, lift them out of the sauce, refrigerate and use for a easy lunch. Double this recipe and steam it in two pans if you have two steamer baskets.

6 chicken thighs, skinned with fat
  removed
2 tbs. dry sherry
2 tbs. hoisin sauce
2 tbs. soy sauce

1 tsp. grated fresh ginger root
1 large clove garlic, minced
3 green onions, with some of green
  leaves, cut in 1-inch pieces

Combine all ingredients except green onions, coating chicken pieces evenly with sauce. Place chicken in an heatproof bowl or pan with sides that will fit into the steamer with enough room for steam to circulate. Top with onion pieces, cover tightly with a lid or foil, and place on steamer rack. When steamer water comes to a boil, steam for 40 to 45 minutes, or until juices run clear and the internal temperature reaches 160°. Check occasionally to see that there is enough water in bottom of steamer, and add more water when necessary.

CURRIED CHICKEN THIGHS

Servings: 3-4

Serve this savory curry with steamed rice, a fresh fruit salad, a good chutney and sprinkled with chopped peanuts or almonds, shredded plain coconut and raisins.

2 tbs. butter
¾ cup chopped onion
1 tbs. curry powder or to taste
1 small tart cooking apple, peeled, cored
1 small baking potato, peeled

1 small carrot, peeled and diced
6 boneless, skinless chicken thighs, cut in half
1 tbs. lemon juice
¼ tsp. thyme
salt and freshly ground pepper

Sauté onion in butter for 3 to 4 minutes. Add curry powder to skillet and cook for another 2 to 3 minutes. Chop apple and potato into ½-inch pieces. Place apple, potato and carrot in bottom of a heatproof bowl that will fit into steamer. Add chicken pieces; sprinkle with lemon juice, thyme, salt and pepper. Spoon curried onion mixture over chicken, spreading some on each piece. When steamer water comes to a boil, place chicken on steamer rack, cover steamer and steam for about 35 minutes, until chicken is tender. Remove chicken from sauce and keep warm. Pour sauce ingredients in the bowl of a food processor and process until smooth. Combine with chicken and serve hot.

STEAMED RICE

Rice takes a little longer to steam than to cook on the top of the stove. If you have a large steamer, or two steaming racks, it will steam in about the same amount of time as an entrée. Use a little less water because it will absorb some extra liquid from the steaming process.

1 cup long grain rice
1½ cups water
salt

Combine rice, water and salt in a heatproof bowl. Place on steamer rack and steam for about 30 minutes after steamer water comes to a boil.

CHICKEN BREASTS MILANO

Servings: 2

Chicken breasts steam quickly with strips of roasted red peppers and a slice of Fontina cheese.

2 boneless skinless chicken breasts
salt and pepper
2-3 fresh basil leaves, slivered or 1/8 tsp. dried
6-8 strips roasted red peppers
2-4 thin slices ripe Italian plum tomato
4 thin slices Fontina cheese

Slightly flatten chicken breasts between sheets of waxed paper, sprinkle with salt and pepper and place on a small plate that has been sprayed with nonstick cooking spray. Top each chicken breast with half of the sweet basil, red peppers, tomatoes and cheese. Cover plate with plastic wrap or invert another slightly larger plate over chicken. Steam 8 to 9 minutes after steamer water comes to a boil, or until chicken is slightly springy to the touch. Serve immediately.

CHICKEN BREASTS WITH PEANUT SAUCE   Servings: 2

Chicken breasts are coated with a slightly spicy peanut sauce and steamed for a quick entrée.

2 skinless boneless chicken breasts
2 tbs. peanut butter
1 tbs. soy sauce
2 tsp. brown sugar
1 tbs. rice wine vinegar
1/2 tsp. Dijon mustard

1/2 tsp. grated fresh ginger root
several drops Tabasco Sauce
1/2 tsp. sesame oil
1 green onion, cut into slivers
fresh cilantro leaves for garnish

Slightly flatten chicken breasts between two sheets of waxed paper. Place on a small plate that has been sprayed with nonstick cooking spray. Combine remaining ingredients except for onion and cilantro leaves, and spread over chicken breasts. Top with onion slivers and cover plate with plastic wrap or invert a slightly larger plate over chicken. When steamer water boils, steam chicken 8 to 9 minutes, or until chicken is slightly springy to the touch. Garnish with cilantro leaves and serve immediately with steamed rice and a green vegetable.

CHICKEN BREASTS WITH MUSTARD

Salt and pepper flattened boneless chicken breasts and spread with a mixture of equal parts of Dijon mustard and plain yogurt. Sprinkle with 1 tsp. minced fresh or dried chives. Cover and steam as directed on page 96.

CHICKEN BREASTS WITH CREAMED SPINACH

Salt and pepper flattened boneless chicken breasts and spread top with 1/4 of a package of defrosted creamed spinach. Cover and steam as directed on page 96.

CHICKEN BREASTS WITH PESTO

Coat flattened boneless chicken breasts with pesto sauce, cover and steam as directed on page 96. Garnish with toasted pine nuts, Parmesan cheese and a fresh, peeled, seeded and chopped tomato.

TUNA SAUCE FOR TURKEY OR CHICKEN Makes: 2 cups

This is a savory mayonnaise sauce for cooked turkey or chicken white meat. Slice meat about 1/4-inch thick and arrange on a platter. Spread slices with the tuna sauce and garnish with strips of roasted red pepper and some black olives. Serve as an appetizer, luncheon entrée or as part of a buffet.

1 egg
1½ tbs. lemon juice
½ tsp. salt
generous amounts of white pepper
dash Tabasco Sauce
1 cup light olive oil
1 can (6½ oz.) tuna with oil
4-5 flat anchovies, rinsed and chopped

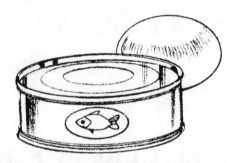

Place egg, lemon juice, salt, pepper and Tabasco in a blender container or food processor bowl; process 30 to 45 seconds. At low speed, slowly pour in oil. When mixture starts to thicken, add tuna and anchovies; process until smooth. Refrigerate until ready to serve. One cup of sauce will coat about 15 slices.

MEAT

It is easy to make savory meat dishes in the steamer. It is not necessary to brown the meat before steaming, particularly when cooking the meat with a flavorful sauce. Any dish that can be braised in the oven adapts easily to the steamer and generally cooks either in the same amount or less time. For recipes with long cooking times, be sure to check the water level in the steamer, adding more water as it becomes necessary.

The hearty *Lamb Shanks with Garlic and Onions*, *Chile Verde*, *Brisket Mexicana, and Belgian Beef Stew* all make wonderful winter dinners. Several recipes for stuffed vegetables are included in this section. The *Stuffed Cabbage Leaves* can be done ahead and frozen, if desired. There are *Savory Swiss Chard Bundles* filled with bulghur and mushrooms, and the *Turkish-Style Stuffed Eggplant* combines the wonderful mint and spices of the Middle East with lamb and onions.

LAMB SHANKS WITH GARLIC AND ONIONS

This is a wonderful cold night dinner. Accompany the savory lamb shanks with mashed potatoes, cooked pasta or rice to absorb the full-flavored sauce. Steam in a heatproof container with sides that will fit in the steamer.

4 lamb shanks, about 3 lbs., trimmed
  of all fat
2 cloves garlic, thinly sliced
2 tbs. olive oil
1 large onion, thinly sliced

⅓ cup red wine
⅓ cup beef broth
1 tbs. tomato paste
1 tbs. soy sauce
½ tsp. thyme

Cut two small slits in each trimmed lamb shank and insert thin slices of garlic. Heat olive oil in a medium skillet and brown lamb shanks on each side. Place in steaming dish. Sauté onion slices in same skillet for 3 to 4 minutes until soft, add remaining garlic slivers and continue to cook for another 2 to 3 minutes. Add remaining ingredients, bring to a boil and pour over lamb shanks. Place lamb shanks in steamer when water is boiling, cover steamer and steam for about 1¾ to 2 hours. Check water level in steamer, adding more when needed. Serve 1 lamb shank per person with potatoes, rice or pasta. The cooking liquid can be strained, degreased and reduced if desired.

MEXICAN BURRITOS

Servings: 4-6

Mexican-style burritos are delicious and very easy to make in a steamer. Serve with hot fresh tortillas garnished with cilantro, avocado, and salsa.

2-2½ lbs. boned pork shoulder
2½ tbs. prepared chili powder
flour tortillas

avocado, diced
fresh cilantro leaves

Cut boned pork shoulder into 2½-inch pieces. Rub on all sides with prepared chili powder. Spray an ovenproof pan with nonstick cooking spray and arrange pork cubes in pan with a little room between pieces. When water is boiling, place pan into steamer, cover and steam for about 45 minutes, or until the internal temperature reaches 160°. Remove from steamer and allow to cool slightly.

Preheat oven to 450°. Place meat pieces on a rack on a baking sheet and bake for 10 to 15 minutes just to crisp up outside of meat. Heat tortillas in foil in oven at the same time. Thinly slice meat and place on a serving platter with diced avocado and fresh cilantro. Pass hot tortillas and fresh salsa. Place some meat, avocado and cilantro in middle of tortilla, fold up bottom edge, fold over side edges to make a fat roll, and start eating from open top edge.

BOB'S DAD'S BEEF STEW

This is more like an extra chunky soup with its wonderful beefy broth. If you have a large steamer, double the recipe. This can be made ahead and refrigerated for a couple of days before reheating and serving.

1 lb. lean stewing beef, cut into
  1½-inch cubes
salt, pepper and flour
2 tsp. vegetable oil
1 can (14½ oz.) beef broth
1 large red or white boiling potato,
  cut into 1-inch cubes
1 small turnip, peeled and cut into
  1-inch cubes

1 small onion, peeled and cut into
  quarters
1 tender rib celery, coarsely chopped
2 large carrots, peeled and cut lengthwise into ½-inch by 2-inch pieces
salt and freshly ground pepper

Dry beef chunks on a paper towel, salt and pepper generously and sprinkle with flour. Heat 2 tsp. oil in a large nonstick skillet. Brown beef pieces on all sides over high heat. Place in steamer bowl with remaining ingredients. Cover steamer, bring water to a boil and steam for 1½ hours. Check water level in steamer, adding more if necessary during steaming process. When meat is tender, carefully remove from steamer and serve in soup bowls.

STEAMED MUSHROOM BEEF

This low fat savory meat dish is flavored with Chinese dried mushrooms. Add some defrosted frozen peas just before steaming for pretty color. For variety, stir in ½ cup sour cream or yogurt before serving over rice or noodles.

½ lb. flank steak, cut in ½-inch by
  2-inch slices across the grain
5-6 medium sized dried shiitaki
  mushrooms
1 tbs. oyster sauce
1 tsp. soy sauce
¼ tsp. sesame oil

1 tbs. cornstarch
1 tbs. dry sherry
2-3 green onions, thinly sliced
½ cup defrosted peas
1 tbs. minced fresh ginger root
fresh cilantro for garnish

Soak mushrooms in hot water for 20 minutes until soft, squeeze dry and cut out hard stems. Slice into thin slivers. Marinate steak with oyster and soy sauce, sesame oil, cornstarch and sherry for 30 minutes, stirring once or twice. Coat with nonstick spray a 8- or 9-inch cake pan or pie plate that fits into the steamer. Combine beef with mushrooms, onions, peas and fresh ginger and spread in pan in an even layer. When steamer water has come to a boil, steam for 6 minutes. Carefully remove from steamer, pour into a serving bowl and garnish with fresh cilantro leaves.

BRISKET MEXICANA

*Beef brisket steams to tenderness in a spicy salsa. Accompany with **Steamer Polenta**, page 34. If you have a two-tiered steamer, the polenta can be added the last 45 minutes the brisket is steaming. This also makes wonderful sandwiches.*

2 lbs. beef brisket, well trimmed
1 tbs. chili powder
1 onion, thinly sliced
1 can (14½ oz.) ready-made salsa, or 1½ cups prepared salsa

Rub both sides of brisket with chili powder. Place brisket in an ovenproof dish or 8- or 9-inch pan sprayed with nonstick cooking spray that fits into the steamer. Top with sliced onions and salsa. Cover pan with 2 layers of foil and place in steamer rack when steamer water has come to a boil. Steam for 3 hours, checking from time to time to see if more water is needed in steamer. Carefully remove from steamer, thinly slice if serving immediately and top with some sauce. The brisket can be refrigerated in its cooking liquid and reheated when ready to serve.

OSSO BUCCO

*This is comfort food. Succulent veal shanks cook in a savory sauce to be spooned over hot rice or **Steamer Polenta**, page 34. Use rosemary instead of thyme for a variation.*

2 tbs. olive oil
2 lb. veal shanks, cut into 1½-inch pieces
salt, pepper and flour
2 large onions, thinly sliced
1 large carrot, coarsely grated
2 cloves garlic, minced
1 cup beef broth or dry white wine
1 tbs. tomato paste
½ tsp. dried thyme or 1 tsp. fresh

Heat 1 tbs. of olive oil in a large skillet. Salt, pepper and flour veal shanks, and then brown on all sides in olive oil. Remove and place in a heatproof dish or 8x8-inch pan with high sides just large enough to hold veal in 1 layer. Add remaining tablespoon of oil to skillet and sauté onions, carrot and garlic over low heat for 6 to 8 minutes until onions are soft and golden. Add beef broth, tomato paste and thyme to skillet, bring to a boil, and pour over veal shanks. Cover pan with foil and place on a steamer rack in steamer. When steamer water comes to a boil, steam for 1¾ hours, until veal is tender. Check water level in steamer, adding more when necessary. Serve immediately with hot rice or polenta. Sprinkle with *Gremolata* if desired.

GREMOLATA
lemon zest from 1 lemon
1 clove of garlic
2 tbs. Italian parsley

Mince lemon zest, garlic and parsley together very finely.

CHINESE-STYLE SAVORY MINCED PORK

Servings: 4

This dish is a Chinese-style meat loaf formed into one large patty or 4 smaller ones. Serve it with hot steamed rice to soak up the flavorful juices.

1 lb. ground pork
¼ cup diced water chestnuts
2 tbs. soy sauce
1 egg, lightly beaten
2 tsp. cornstarch
generous amount of white pepper
½ tsp. sesame oil
a few drops of hot pepper sauce, if desired

Combine all ingredients and pat into an 8-inch pie plate or other heatproof dish with sides if making 1 large patty, or form into 4 individual patties. Place plate on steamer rack and steam for 35 minutes after water has come to a boil. Serve hot over steamed rice, with snow peas or broccoli.

CHILE VERDE

Pork tenderloin pieces simmer with green chiles, tomatoes and cilantro to make a flavorful stew. This goes together quickly and you don't have to brown the meat.

1½ lbs. pork tenderloin
1 large onion, chopped
2 cloves garlic, peeled and chopped
1 bay leaf
½ tsp. salt
freshly ground black pepper

1½ cups chicken broth
¼ tsp. oregano
¾ cup chopped tomato, fresh or canned
1 can (7 oz.) diced green chiles
1 tbs. chopped cilantro

Cut meat into 1-inch pieces and place in a heatproof bowl. Add onion, garlic, bay leaf, salt, pepper and chicken broth. Cover with tight fitting lid or aluminum foil and place on steamer rack in steamer. When steamer water boils, steam for 1 hour. Check water level in steamer, adding more when necessary. Stir once during steaming. After 1 hour carefully remove cover and stir in oregano, tomatoes, green chiles and chopped cilantro. Re-cover and steam for 30 minutes longer. Taste and add hot sauce if desired. Serve immediately in shallow soup bowls with fresh flour tortillas or rice, or make into burritos, adding a little shredded Monterey Jack cheese and fresh cilantro.

BELGIAN BEEF STEW

Servings: 4

You don't have to brown the meat and onions first, but it adds a lot of flavor and makes a more attractive dish. If you have room, steam small new potatoes and some cabbage in a second layer to make a complete meal.

2 lbs. top round steak, cut into 1-1½-inch cubes
salt, pepper and flour
¼ cup olive oil
2 large onions, thinly sliced
2 large garlic cloves, minced
1½ cups full-bodied beer
2 tbs. white or red wine vinegar
2 tbs. chopped fresh sage leaves, or ½ tsp. dried
salt and freshly ground pepper
1 tbs. butter blended with 1 tbs. flour to thicken sauce
20 small new potatoes, optional
1 small head cabbage, outer leaves removed, cut into quarters, optional

Heat oil in a large skillet. Salt and pepper beef cubes, roll in flour and brown on all sides over medium high heat. Remove cubes to a large heatproof bowl that will fit into steamer. Add onions and garlic to skillet, scraping up any browned bits, and sauté 5 to 6 minutes until onions are softened and translucent. Pour in beer and vinegar, bring to a boil and pour over meat. Add sage, salt and pepper. Cover bowl with foil or a tight fitting lid and place on steamer rack. When steamer water comes to a boil, place rack in steamer and steam for 1 hour. Check water level in steamer, adding more when necessary. Carefully remove from steamer and pour off liquid through a strainer into a saucepan. Place saucepan over medium heat and bring to a boil. Gradually add bits of flour-butter mixture, stirring until sauce thickens. Pour sauce back over meat and onions and serve immediately.

If steaming potatoes and cabbage to go with meat, about 35 minutes before meat is done, add small new potatoes to steamer, either in a separate layer or around meat, if there is room. When you strain meat juices to thicken them, place cabbage wedges in steamer and steam for 6 to 8 minutes, until just tender-crisp.

STUFFED CABBAGE LEAVES

Makes: 16-18

This recipe takes a little time to put together but it can be made ahead and freezes beautifully. Buy the largest head of cabbage you can find for large leaves. If you run out of large leaves, just put two smaller ones together.

2 heads cabbage
1 tbs. olive oil
1 cup onions, finely chopped
1 clove garlic, minced
½ lb. lean ground beef
½ lb. lean ground pork
2 tbs. chopped parsley
salt, pepper and a few grinds of nutmeg
1 cup cooked rice

1¾ cups beef broth
2 tbs. tomato paste
1 can (14 oz.) tomato pieces with juice
6-8 drops Tabasco Sauce
½ tsp. dried sweet basil
2 tbs. lemon juice
2 tbs. flour
¼ cup sour cream

Bring a large pot of water to a boil. Core cabbage and place in boiling water. Let stand for 10 minutes. Remove cabbage and when cool enough to handle, gently pull off large outer leaves. If inside leaves are not pliable, return cabbage to hot water and let stand until leaves soften. Cut out large ribs from stem end of leaves. Place rib pieces and some small leaves of cabbage in the bottom of a heatpoof baking pan. You will need two 8x8-inch pans or similar size heatproof dishes with sides, and depending on the size of your steamer, the cabbage rolls may be steamed in two batches.

Heat oil in a small skillet and sauté onion 3 to 4 minutes. Add garlic and cook for another minute. Allow to cool slightly before combining with ground meats, parsley, salt, pepper, nutmeg and rice. Mix well. Place about 2 table-spoons of filling on each cabbage leaf at stem end.

Fold sides of leaf over filling and roll up into a neat package. Place rolls seam side down over cabbage pieces, fitting them closely together. Combine beef broth, tomato paste and pieces, Tabasco, sweet basil and lemon juice. Pour over rolls. Cover rolls with additional small cabbage leaves, if available. Place on steamer rack and when steamer water comes to a boil, cover steamer and steam 1 hour. Check water level in steamer, adding more when necessary.

Combine sour cream and flour. Allow to stand at room temperature until cabbage rolls are cooked. Carefully remove cabbage rolls to a serving plate and keep warm. Pour pan juices through a strainer into the bowl of a food processor. Discard cabbage pieces, but add tomato pieces to sauce with sour cream and flour mixture. Process until smooth and well blended. Pour into a saucepan and heat over low heat until sauce thickens. Pour over cabbage rolls and serve immediately.

TURKISH-STYLE STUFFED EGGPLANT   Servings: 4-6

Depending on your appetite and the size of the eggplants, this recipe can be a substantial main course by itself or cut into pieces for smaller servings to accompany other dishes. This recipe can also be cut in half and done in a smaller steamer.

2 eggplants, ¾-1 lb. each
2 tbs. full-flavored olive oil
½ lb. ground lamb or beef
½ cup minced onion
½ cup chopped tomatoes
¼ cup minced parsley
¼ cup minced mint leaves

2 tbs. lemon juice
½ tsp. cinnamon
½ tsp. allspice
dash nutmeg
salt and freshly ground pepper
¼ cup toasted pine nuts or almonds

Cut stem end off eggplants and cut eggplants in half lengthwise. Hollow out each half, leaving about ½-inch-thick shell. Chop eggplant pulp into ½-inch pieces. Heat oil in a large skillet and sauté lamb with onions and eggplant pulp until meat is browned and eggplant is soft, 8 to 10 minutes. Combine with remaining ingredients and mix well. Stuff mixture into eggplant shells, place shells on one or two heatproof plates and place on a steamer rack. When steamer water comes to a boil, place rack in steamer and steam, covered, for

20 minutes until eggplant shells are soft and can be easily pierced with a sharp knife. Carefully remove eggplants from steamer and place on serving plates. Serve with *Easy Tomato Sauce*.

EASY TOMATO SAUCE
1 cup crushed tomatoes, or canned tomato pieces chopped in a food processor
2 tsp. brown sugar
½ tsp. dried sweet basil
salt and freshly ground pepper
6-8 drops Tabasco Sauce

Combine ingredients in a small saucepan, bring to a boil and simmer over low heat about 5 minutes, until sauce thickens slightly. Spoon over stuffed eggplants.

SAVORY SWISS CHARD BUNDLES

Makes: 8-10

Large red Swiss chard leaves are filled with lamb, mushrooms and bulghur. Serve as an entrée with Greek Lemon Sauce.

about 15 large red Swiss chard leaves
1 cup cooked bulghur, recipe follows
3 tbs. full-flavored olive oil
3/4 cup finely chopped onions
1/2 lb. mushrooms, finely chopped
1 clove garlic, minced

1/2 lb. ground lamb or beef
2 tbs. lemon juice
1/2 tsp. thyme
2 tbs. minced parsley
Greek Lemon Sauce, recipe follows

Soften chard leaves by dipping them one at a time in boiling water for about 15 seconds to soften. Kitchen tongs work well for this. Remove leaves and spread out on paper towels.

Heat olive oil in a medium skillet and sauté onions, mushrooms and garlic for 5 to 6 minutes until onions are soft and mushroom liquid has evaporated. Allow to cool slightly before combining with remaining ingredients.

To assemble: Cut chard leaves in half lengthwise, removing tough center stems. Cut each long half horizontally so you have two pieces about the same size. Place leaves side by side, overlapping in the middle. Place about 1/3 cup of filling in center of each leaf, bringing up sides to enclose filling. Place rolls seam side down in an oiled heatproof baking dish, as close together as possible. You may need two pans, depending on the size of your steamer. Cover rolls with any extra chard leaves and place dish on a steamer rack. When steamer water boils, steam rolls for 45 minutes. Carefully remove from steamer and place rolls on serving plates. Serve immediately with *Greek Lemon Sauce.*

STEAMED BULGHUR

Makes: 1½ cups

½ cup bulghur   salt
1 cup chicken stock

Combine bulghur with stock and salt in a small bowl. Place on steamer rack; when steamer water comes to a boil, steam for 15 minutes.

GREEK LEMON SAUCE

1 tbs. lemon juice   1 egg
1 tsp. cornstarch   ¾ cup chicken stock

Dissolve cornstarch in lemon juice. Beat egg with lemon juice and add cooking liquid or chicken stock. Heat over low heat until sauce is hot, but do not boil. Serve immediately.

APRICOT-STUFFED PORK TENDERLOINS   Servings: 3-4

This is an elegant dinner entrée, or makes delicious sandwiches if there is any left over. You could also stuff the tenderloins with dried prunes for a variation.

6-8 dried apricots
2 small pork tenderloins, about 1 lb. total
1 tbs. butter
2 tbs. finely chopped onion
⅛ tsp. thyme
⅛ tsp. dried sweet basil
salt and freshly ground pepper

Cover apricots with hot water and allow to stand 15 minutes to soften. Butterfly tenderloins by cutting each down center to within ½-inch of cutting completely through meat. Open up like a book and flatten slightly with a meat mallet. Sauté onion in butter for 4 to 5 minutes to soften. Add thyme and basil. Drain apricots and cut into thin strips. Combine with onion. Salt and pepper tenderloins. Spread filling down center of one tenderloin and top with the other piece of meat, placing narrow end at wide end of bottom tenderloin. Fold meat around stuffing and tie in several places to hold meat in place.

Spray a small plate with nonstick cooking spray and place meat on plate. Place a rack in the steamer and place plate on rack. When steamer water boils, time steaming for about 35 minutes or until internal temperature of meat reaches 160°. Carefully remove from steamer and allow to set up for 10 minutes before slicing and serving. This is also good served cold. Remove from the refrigerator about 20 minutes before serving.

EGGS

Gentle steaming is an excellent method for cooking eggs and quickly produces delicious poached, soft or hard boiled eggs. *Chawan-Mushi* is a savory Japanese-style custard with dried Shiitaki mushrooms, scallops and shrimp. The *Crustless Onion Quiche* is steamed in individual custard cups and has the classic flavors of Gruyère cheese and bacon. Try steaming eggs for *Mexican-Style Eggs* or other favorites, such as Eggs Benedict.

CHAWAN-MUSHI

This is a delicate Japanese-style shrimp and scallop custard. It makes a special brunch or light supper entrée.

2 small dried Shiitaki mushrooms
4 small fresh green beans
3 large eggs
1 cup chicken broth
1 tsp. soy sauce

1 tbs. dry sherry
salt and white pepper
8 small bay scallops
4 medium sized shrimp, peeled and
   deveined

Place dried mushrooms and green beans in a small bowl, cover with boiling water and allow to stand for 15 minutes. Drain, remove green beans and set aside. Squeeze mushrooms dry and cut out tough stems. Slice into thin slivers. In a mixing bowl, beat eggs with a fork until well combined but not frothy. Stir in chicken broth, soy sauce, sherry, salt and pepper. Spray four 1-cup custard cups or small soufflé dishes with nonstick cooking spray. Arrange shrimp, scallops, green beans and mushroom slices in bottom of cups. Pour egg mixture through a sieve into cups, filling them equally. Cover each cup with aluminum foil and place on a steamer rack. When steamer water comes to a boil, carefully place rack in steamer, cover and steam for 20 minutes. Custards are done when a knife blade comes out clean. Serve immediately in cups.

EGGS

If you want hard boiled, soft boiled or poached eggs, consider using the steamer. A trick to keep eggs from cracking is to make a small hole with a pin on the rounded end of each egg before cooking. Start eggs with cold water in the steamer and then time them to the desired doneness when the water comes to a full boil.

HARD BOILED EGGS

Place eggs on a steamer plate in the steamer, add about 1 cup water, cover steamer and cook 14 to 16 minutes after water boils. Remove eggs and immediately plunge into a bowl of cold water to cool.

SOFT BOILED EGGS

Place eggs on a steamer plate in the steamer, add about ¾ cup water, cover steamer and cook about 8 minutes after water boils. Remove and serve hot.

POACHED EGGS

Spray small custard cups or ramekins with nonstick cooking spray. Break 1 egg in each cup; season with salt and pepper, and add a sliver of butter if desired. Add 1 to 2 cups water to steamer, and place steamer rack with custard cups in steamer. Cover steamer, bring water to a boil, and steam until eggs reach desired firmness. Soft poached eggs generally cook in 5 to 6 minutes, and firmer eggs in 7 to 8 minutes. Carefully remove egg cups from steamer, run the thin blade of a knife around the edge and slide eggs onto individual warm serving plates, or onto buttered toast. Serve immediately.

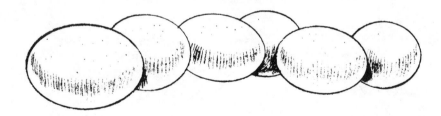

MEXICAN-STYLE EGGS

Servings: 2-4

Poached eggs are served on a hot corn tortilla topped with a spicy tomato sauce, cheese and cilantro. Consider serving two eggs and tortillas for those with heartier appetites.

SAUCE

2 tbs. vegetable oil
1/3 cup finely chopped onion
2 cups canned crushed tomatoes
1/2 cup diced canned green chiles

1/4 tsp. oregano
1/2 tsp. cumin
salt and pepper
Tabasco Sauce to taste

FOR EACH SERVING

1-2 corn tortillas
2-3 tbs. shredded Monterey Jack
  cheese
1-2 poached eggs, page 123

fresh cilantro leaves
sliced black olives or avocado slices
  for garnish, optional

124 EGGS

Heat 1 tbs. oil in a medium skillet. Sauté onion for 3 to 4 minutes until soft. Add tomatoes, green chiles, oregano, cumin, salt, pepper and hot sauce. Bring to a boil and simmer 3 to 4 minutes to thicken sauce.

In another skillet, heat remaining oil and quickly heat tortillas, one at a time, to soften.

To assemble: Place a tortilla on a warm plate and top with a small amount of tomato sauce. Slide a poached egg onto sauce, and spoon a little more tomato sauce over egg. Sprinkle with cheese and fresh cilantro leaves. Garnish if desired and serve immediately.

CRUSTLESS ONION QUICHE

This is a delicious creamy classic onion and bacon quiche. Serve hot or warm as an entrée for a lunch or supper with a crisp green salad.

4 slices bacon, cut into ½-inch pieces
1 large yellow onion, thinly sliced
2 eggs
1 cup half and half
⅓ cup shredded Gruyère cheese

⅓ cup grated Parmesan cheese
dash of nutmeg
salt, freshly ground pepper and a few
  drops of Tabasco Sauce

Sauté bacon pieces in a skillet until cooked but not crisp. Remove bacon pieces from pan and reserve. Pour out all but 1 tbs. of bacon fat from skillet. Slowly cook onions in skillet until soft and lightly golden, about 15 minutes. Remove from heat and allow to cool slightly before adding to egg mixture. Whisk eggs and half and half in a small bowl until well blended. Stir in bacon, onions, cheeses, nutmeg, salt, pepper and Tabasco. Spray four 6-oz. soufflé or custard cups with nonstick spray, or butter generously. Divide mixture into cups and cover each cup with a piece of foil, crimping foil around edge of cups. Place a steamer rack in bottom of steamer with 1 to 2 cups water. When water comes to a boil, carefully place cups on rack, cover steamer and steam for about 25 to 30 minutes. Quiche will be done when centers puff slightly and a knife blade comes out clean.

DIM SUM FAVORITES

A steamer is the ideal way to reheat the Chinese steamed buns and filled wrappers that you find in the market or Chinese take-out counters. Many of the flavorful small Asian appetizer dishes are steamed.

Included in this section are some dim sum delights that go together quickly and when served together can make a complete light lunch or a sumptuous appetizer party.

PAPER-WRAPPED SALMON

Makes: 12 pieces

Marinated strips of fresh salmon are wrapped in foil and quickly steamed. These can be made ahead, refrigerated and steamed just before serving. Give each person a small plate to collect the juices and wrappers.

1 lb. salmon fillet
½ tsp. grated fresh ginger root
1 tbs. soy sauce
1 tbs. dry sherry or Shao Xing rice wine
1 tbs. oyster sauce
1 tsp. sesame oil
1 tsp. cornstarch
2-3 green onions, cut into long slivers
fresh cilantro leaves
12 pieces of foil, each about 5 inches square

Remove skin from salmon and cut into 12 finger-size pieces about ½-inch x 2 inches long. Combine ginger, soy sauce, sherry, oyster sauce, sesame oil and cornstarch; toss with salmon pieces. Marinate for about 15 minutes. Place a drained piece of salmon just below center of the foil square. Top with slivers of onion and 2 to 3 fresh cilantro leaves. Bring top half of foil piece down over salmon even with bottom edge of foil. Fold up about ¼-inch from bottom and then make a fold ¼-inch in from each side. Continue to fold up bottom and side edges until you can feel that you are close to salmon piece inside foil. Place foil packets on a collapsible steamer basket or rack, allowing room for steam to circulate around packages. Place about 1 cup of water in steamer. When water boils, lower steamer basket into steamer, cover and cook for 7 minutes. Remove packets from steamer and serve hot.

VARIATIONS

- Cut fresh snow peas into thin long slivers and place on top of salmon before steaming.

- Marinate peeled large shrimp (31 to 40 count per lb.) or tiger prawns instead of salmon. If using smaller shrimp, place 2 to 3 in each package.

STEAMED DUCK BUNS

These Chinese-style steamed buns are filled with cooked duck and plum sauce. The bun dough goes together quickly in the food processor. These can be made ahead and then steamed for 2 minutes to reheat. They also freeze well.

1 cup all purpose flour
1 cup cake flour
2 tbs. sugar
2½ tsp. baking powder
1 tbs. vegetable shortening
⅔ cup milk
¾ cup cooked duck, cut into ⅜-inch cubes
⅓ cup plum sauce or hoisin sauce
2 green onions, white part only, minced
8 foil pieces about 2 inches square

Add flours, sugar and baking powder to food processor bowl. Pulse to mix well. Add shortening and pulse several times to combine. With processor running, add milk and process until dough forms a ball. Turn out dough onto a lightly floured board and knead for 1 to 2 minutes. Dough will be quite soft. Form dough into a log about 12 inches long. Cover with plastic wrap and allow to rest while preparing filling. Combine duck pieces with plum sauce and green onions.

To form buns, cut dough into 8 equal pieces. Take a piece of dough and flatten into a 3- to 4-inch circle, thicker in middle than on edges. Put about 2 tbs. filling in middle of circle and pull up sides of dough. Pleat and pinch dough to seal top. Place each bun on a square of aluminum foil and arrange on a steamer plate. Depending on the size of your steamer, you may want to steam these in two batches.

Place a platform to support a steamer plate about 2 inches above water in bottom of steamer. Add 3 to 4 cups water to steamer and bring to a boil. When water boils, carefully place steamer plate with buns on steamer rack. Cover steamer and steam for 10 minutes. Remove cooked buns with kitchen tongs. Repeat steaming process with remaining buns if doing 2 batches. Serve at warm or at room temperature. Steam to reheat.

SHRIMP AND SCALLOP SHAO MAI

Makes: 16-18

A shrimp and scallop filling is steamed in round noodle wrappers. If you can't find the round wrappers, cut square won ton wrappers into 3-inch circles. Depending the size of your steamer, you may want to steam these in two batches.

FILLING

½ lb. shrimp, peeled, deveined
¼ lb. scallops
6 water chestnuts
2 green onions, white part only,
  finely minced

1 tsp. grated fresh ginger root
1 tbs. oyster sauce
salt and white pepper

FOR ASSEMBLY

3-inch round shao mai wrappers

fresh cilantro leaves

DIPPING SAUCE

hot pepper oil
rice wine vinegar

soy sauce

If preparing by hand, all ingredients including shrimp and scallops should be finely chopped and then combined. If using the food processor, mince water chestnuts, onions and ginger and then add remaining ingredients, pulsing a few times to chop. Ingredients should be in small chunks. Do not overprocess.

To assemble: Place about a tablespoon of mixture in center of wrapper. Bring sides of wrapper up around filling, pleating wrapper a little to form a cup. The finished shao mai will look like a tiny cupcake showing shrimp filling in center. Place a fresh cilantro leaf over meat. Keep unused wrappers covered with a damp paper towel so they don't dry out.

To steam: Place 2 to 3 cups of water in a steamer. Place a small platform to hold steamer plate above water. Spray steamer plate with nonstick cooking spray and arrange shao mai on plate about 1 inch apart. When water is steaming, carefully lower plate and place on rack in steamer. Cover steamer and steam for 15 minutes. Remove shao mai and serve immediately.

To serve: Pour a small amount of rice vinegar, soy sauce, and a few drops of hot pepper oil into small dishes. Dip shao mai into sauce. The cooked shao mai can be refrigerated and reheated in the microwave or steamed for a few minutes. These can also be assembled ahead, covered with plastic wrap and refrigerated until steaming. The recipe amounts can easily be doubled.

STEAMED BEEF CILANTRO BALLS

Makes: 20

These Chinese meatballs make a delicious appetizer. Serve with a hot Chinese mustard sauce. These can be made ahead and reheated in the microwave if there are any left over.

½ lb. ground chuck
5 green onions, white part only, minced
¼ cup minced water chestnuts, about 6
1 tsp. minced fresh ginger root
½ tsp. sugar
¼ tsp. salt
1 tsp. soy sauce
1 tbs. oyster sauce
1 tsp. dry sherry
½ tsp. sesame oil
1 egg white
2 tsp. cornstarch
2 tbs. chopped fresh cilantro leaves

Combine all ingredients in a small bowl and form into 1-½ inch balls. Spray a heatproof plate with nonstick cooking spray and arrange meatballs on plate. Place 2 to 3 cups water in steamer and place a small stand or rack in steamer to hold plate above water. When steamer water boils, carefully lower plate onto rack, cover steamer, and steam for 20 minutes. Serve hot with *Chinese-Style Mustard Sauce*.

CHINESE-STYLE MUSTARD SAUCE

You will need Coleman's dry mustard for this sauce. It is quite hot, so use with caution.

2 tbs. Coleman's dry mustard powder
1 tbs. soy sauce
⅛ tsp. sesame oil
⅛ tsp. sugar

Combine all ingredients into a smooth paste. Leftover mustard should be covered and refrigerated.

FRUIT

Steaming is a quick, delicious way to prepare fruit. Here are some easy, low calorie fruit desserts and a great *Chunky Apple Sauce*. Try the *Elegant Stuffed Pears* or the *Peaches with Raspberries* for a delicious summer evening dinner finale. The *Dried Fruit Compote* is nice to keep on hand for nutritious breakfast fare or as part of a bunch buffet. Most of these recipes can be made ahead and are good hot, warm or slightly chilled.

APPLES FILLED WITH NUTS AND RAISINS

Stuffed apples are a favorite winter dessert. They can be filled with all kinds of nuts and spices, eaten hot or cold, plain or topped with ice cream or heavy cream. Apples steam very rapidly and the steaming times vary. Check at about 7 minutes and then continue to steam another 2 to 3 minutes, or until the apple can be pierced easily with a knife blade.

FOR EACH SERVING

1 cooking apple, Rome Beauty or
  Golden Delicious
1 tsp. white or dark raisins

2 tsp. chopped pecans or walnuts
dash cinnamon
1 tsp. maple syrup

Cut out stem of apple and remove core with a melon baller, keeping bottom of apple intact. With a knife, make a thin slit around middle of apple so it does not collapse during steaming. Combine raisins, nuts and cinnamon and fill center of apple. Pour maple syrup over nuts and raisins. Place in a shallow dish on a steamer rack; when water in steamer is boiling, put plate on steamer rack, cover steamer and steam for 7 to 9 minutes, or until apple is tender. Carefully remove from steamer and serve at room temperature or refrigerate if desired.

SPICY ORANGE-FLAVORED APPLES

This is another stuffed apple variation using diced candied orange peel.

FOR EACH SERVING
1 cooking apple, Rome Beauty or Golden Delicious
½ tsp. candied orange peel
2 tsp. chopped walnuts
½ tsp. cinnamon
1 tsp. brown sugar
1 tsp. Triple Sec or orange juice

Cut out stem of apple and remove core with a melon baller, keeping bottom of apple intact. With a knife, make a thin slit around middle of apple so it does not collapse during steaming. Combine remaining ingredients except for Triple Sec and fill center of apple. Pour Triple Sec or orange juice over nut mixture. Place in a shallow dish on a steamer rack and when water in steamer is boiling, put in steamer rack, cover steamer and steam for 7 to 9 minutes, or until apple is tender.

ZINFANDEL APPLES

Servings: 2-4

Here is a quick pretty dessert. The red Zinfandel wine gives the apples a lovely pink color and lots of flavor. Use a shallow dish large enough to hold the apple halves and still leave at least an inch around the edge of the dish for the steam to circulate.

1 or 2 medium cooking apples, Rome Beauty or Golden Delicious
½ cup Zinfandel wine
2 tbs. brown sugar
¼ tsp. cinnamon

Peel apples, cut in half through stems and remove cores. Place core side down in a shallow heatproof dish. Dissolve sugar and cinnamon in wine and pour over apples. When steamer water is boiling, place dish with apples on steamer rack and steam covered for 8 to 10 minutes. Check at 8 minutes and remove when apples can be easily pierced with a knife blade. Carefully remove hot apples from dish and pour wine into a small saucepan. Bring to a boil over high heat and reduce liquid to about half, or ¼ cup. Pour hot liquid over apples. Serve hot, at room temperature or chill in the refrigerator. This is good with vanilla ice cream, frozen yogurt or a little whipped cream.

GINGERED ORANGE SLICES

Servings: 2-3

This refreshing dish is wonderful served icy cold for a light sweet finish to dinner, or as an accompaniment to a spicy curry or main course. Sprinkle with fresh shredded coconut or slivered almonds, if desired.

2 oranges
½ tsp. grated fresh ginger root
1 tbs. Triple Sec or Grand Marnier

With a sharp knife, carefully remove orange peel and white membrane under it. Slice oranges into thin slices and place in a shallow heatproof bowl on a steaming rack in steamer. Sprinkle with grated ginger and Triple Sec. After steamer water comes to a boil, steam covered for 5 minutes. Carefully remove from steamer and allow to cool. Refrigerate until ready to serve.

PEACHES WITH RASPBERRIES

Servings: 3-4

Summer raspberries and peaches are steamed together to make a delicious light dessert. Serve plain or over vanilla ice cream or with a little whipped cream.

2 fresh ripe peaches, peeled, cut in half , seeds removed
½ cup fresh raspberries
1 tbs. brown sugar
2 tbs. Triple Sec or Framboise liqueur

Place 4 peach halves cut-side up on a shallow plate or bowl that will fit in steamer. Sprinkle fresh raspberries over peaches and top with sugar and liqueur. Place dish on steamer rack. After steamer water comes to a boil, check with tip of a knife at 8 minutes to see if peaches are tender. Do not overcook. Remove from steamer and allow to cool before serving.

PEARS IN RED WINE

Servings: 2

If you like the flavors of red wine, cinnamon and cloves, this is a dessert for you. Serve either warm or chilled, with or without ice cream or whipped cream topped with slivered almonds.

1 large cooking pear, Bosc or Anjou
½ cup full-bodied red wine
2 tbs. brown sugar

¼ tsp. cinnamon
2 whole cloves

Peel pear, cut in half and remove core. Combine remaining ingredients in a shallow heatproof dish and add pear, turning once or twice to coat with wine mixture. Place dish on steaming rack. When steamer water comes to a boil, carefully place steaming rack in steamer, cover and steam for 8 to 10 minutes, until pear is just tender when pierced with a knife blade. Carefully remove dish from steamer and allow to cool slightly. Remove pear halves from steaming dish and pour wine mixture into a small saucepan. Bring to a boil over high heat and reduce to about ½ of original volume, or ¼ cup. Pour hot liquid over pear halves. Serve warm or at room temperature, or refrigerate until ready to serve.

ELEGANT STUFFED PEARS

Pears are stuffed with an orange and nut mixture, then steamed. This is a perfect, very light dessert. This recipe can be increased, depending on your steamer capacity.

1 large cooking pear, Bosc or Anjou
1 tbs. chopped pecans
1 tsp. diced candied orange peel

¼ tsp. cinnamon
1 tsp. brown sugar
2 tbs. Triple Sec or Grand Marnier

Peel pear, cut in half and remove core. Place cut side up in a shallow heatproof dish on a steaming rack. Combine nuts, orange peel and spices, and fill centers of pears. Drizzle 1 tbs. Triple Sec over pear tops and pour remaining tablespoon in bottom of dish. When steamer water comes to a boil, carefully place steaming rack in steamer and steam covered for about 8 minutes, or until pears are just tender when pierced with the blade of a knife. Carefully remove pears from steamer and allow to cool. Serve at room temperature or chilled, if desired.

DRIED FRUIT COMPOTE

Servings: 4

Dried fruits make a flavorful melange for breakfast, brunch or a winter evening dessert. Use a combination of fruits you like. This is good by itself or used as an ice cream topping.

½ cup dried pears or peaches
½ cup dried apricots
½ cup small dried, pitted prunes
¼ cup cranberries
¼ cup dried cherries or raisins

¼ cup brown sugar
1 tbs. lemon juice
1 cup orange juice
½ cup water, or to make enough
  liquid to cover fruit

Cut larger fruits into 1-inch square pieces and combine with sugar and lemon juice in a small heatproof bowl. Add orange juice to just cover fruit and place bowl on a steamer rack. When steamer water comes to a boil, carefully place bowl in steamer, and steam covered for about 20 minutes or until fruit is tender when pierced with a knife. Carefully remove from steamer and allow to cool. Serve warm, at room temperature or chilled, as desired.

CHUNKY APPLE SAUCE

Servings: 3-4

This is a wonderful quick applesauce. Use two different kinds of apples, one sweet and one a tart cooking apple for a homemade treat that is much better than you can get from a jar or tin.

4 apples, 2 Golden Delicious,
  2 McIntosh or other combination
1 tbs. lemon juice
1/3 cup sugar

1 slice fresh ginger root, about the
  size of a quarter
pinch of ground cloves
1/8 tsp. cinnamon

Peel and core apples, cut into quarters and then cut each quarter into 4 or 5 pieces. You want chunks that are approximately the same size. Combine apples with lemon juice and sugar in a heatproof bowl that will fit into your steamer. Add slice of ginger. Place on a steamer rack. When steamer water comes to a boil, place steamer rack in steamer, cover and steam for 15 to 20 minutes until apples are tender. Check at 15 minutes. Carefully remove from steamer and stir in cloves and cinnamon. Allow to cool slightly before serving warm, or refrigerate and serve chilled. Remove ginger slice before serving.

PEAR CUSTARDS

Servings: 4

This light fruit dessert is also delicious when made with thinly sliced apples, plums or peaches. Use one large or two small pieces of fruit. Serve warm with a little whipped cream or ice cream, if desired.

1 egg
1/3 cup sour cream
3 tbs. sugar
1 tbs. flour
1 tsp. vanilla

salt
dash nutmeg
1 large ripe pear, Anjou, Bartlett,
  Bosc or other

Spray 4 custard cups with nonstick cooking spray. Beat together egg and sour cream in a small bowl; combine with sugar, flour, vanilla and salt. Spoon a tablespoon of batter in the bottom of each cup. Peel and core pear. Cut into quarters and cut each quarter across the wide part into 1/4-inch slices. Place pear slices in custard cups, dividing evenly. Sprinkle pear with nutmeg. Top with remaining batter. Cover each cup with foil and place on steamer rack. When the steamer water comes to a boil, place rack in steamer, cover, and steam for 25 minutes, or until a knife blade comes out clean. Allow to stand a few minutes before serving.

BREADS

Thinking of a steamer as a moist oven opens up a wide range of possibilities for cooking. Steamed breads and cakes have almost the same texture as baked, but are quite pale in color instead of having the golden crust of an oven-baked bread. Chopped nuts mixed with a little cinnamon makes an attractive topping for most sweet breads. They can also be garnished with powdered sugar or whipped cream. Once sliced, however, it is not obvious that the breads are steamed.

One of the important techniques in steaming breads is to wrap the lid of the steamer with a dish towel so the steaming liquid doesn't drop down onto the bread batter. If your steamer lid is a one-piece domed cover that is not possible to wrap, lay a piece of foil or parchment paper over the pan to keep out most of the water. For recipes requiring long steaming times, check the water level in the steamer every 20 to 30 minutes and add more water when necessary.

PUMPKIN NUT BREAD

1 loaf

This spicy bread is great by itself or toasted for breakfast. Spread it with cream cheese or goat cheese for a lunch box treat.

2 large eggs
½ cup white sugar
¼ cup brown sugar
⅓ cup vegetable oil
1 cup pumpkin puree
1 tsp. vanilla
1½ cups all purpose flour
½ tsp. salt

1 tsp. baking powder
½ tsp. cinnamon
½ tsp. allspice
½ tsp. powdered ginger
¼ tsp. nutmeg
⅛ tsp. cloves
¾ cup chopped pecans or walnuts

Beat eggs with sugars until sugars are dissolved. Add oil, pumpkin puree and vanilla. Sift flour with spices, add to egg mixture and stir to combine. Stir in chopped nuts and pour batter into a 9x5-inch oiled loaf pan or another heatproof dish that fits into steamer. When steamer water boils, place bread on steamer tray, wrap lid of steamer in a dish towel so liquid doesn't drip into bread, cover and steam for 30 to 35 minutes, until a knife comes out clean.

BANANA BREAD

1 loaf

Use really ripe, sweet bananas in this bread. Toast it for breakfast or spread thin slices with cream cheese mixed with chopped dates or dried apricots for lunch or with a cup of tea. For variety, add ½ cup chopped dates to batter.

2 eggs
½ cup sugar
1 cup mashed banana pulp
1 tsp. vanilla
2 tbs. vegetable oil
2 cups all purpose flour

2 tsp. baking powder
½ tsp. salt
¾ cup chopped pecans or walnuts
½ tsp. cinnamon
1 tbs. brown sugar

Combine eggs, sugar, bananas, vanilla and vegetable oil in a bowl and mix well. Sift flour with baking powder and salt and stir into egg-banana mixture. Add ½ cup of chopped nuts. Pour batter into an oiled 9x5-inch loaf pan or another heatproof dish that fits into steamer, and top with remaining ¼ cup nuts mixed with cinnamon and brown sugar. When water in steamer comes to a boil, place loaf pan on steamer rack above water. Wrap steamer lid with a dish towel so steaming liquid doesn't drip onto bread. Steam for 30 to 35 minutes, until bread is springy to the touch and a knife or toothpick comes out clean. Allow to cool in the pan on a rack for 10 to 15 minutes before unmolding.

APPLESAUCE APRICOT BREAD

1 loaf

The applesauce makes a nice moist bread without adding fat. If you wish, substitute raisins or dates for the dried apricots. Instead of one large loaf bake in a 3x5-inch loaf pan and fill 6 foil baking cups for lunch box treats.

½ cup dried apricots, softened in boiling water
1 egg
½ cup brown sugar
1 cup applesauce
¼ cup milk
1 tsp. vanilla
1½ cups flour
½ tsp. salt
2 tsp. baking powder
¼ tsp. nutmeg
1 tsp. cinnamon
1 cup walnuts, chopped
1 tbs. brown sugar

Bring steamer water to a boil. Drain and dry softened apricots and cut into ¼-inch pieces. Beat egg, add brown sugar, applesauce, milk and vanilla. Sift together flour, salt, baking powder, nutmeg and ½ tsp. cinnamon. Add to egg mixture and just combine. Stir in diced apricots and ¾ cup chopped walnuts. Spoon mixture into heatproof pan that fits into steamer, or use baking cups. Mix together remaining ½ tsp. cinnamon, ¼ cup walnuts and brown sugar. Sprinkle over top of batter.

When steamer water is boiling, place bread pans on steamer rack in steamer. Wrap steamer lid with a dish towel to prevent liquid from dripping onto bread. Cover steamer and steam for 30 to 35 minutes, or until a knife blade comes out clean. Steam cupcakes for 25 minutes. Carefully remove from steamer and place on a rack to cool.

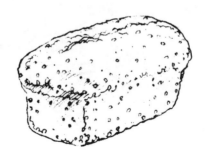

SPICY GINGERBREAD

Servings: 8

This is a delicious spicy gingerbread. If you like a light fluffy-type cake, just steam it uncovered with the steamer lid wrapped in a towel. If you prefer a more dense cake, cover the cake pan with foil and steam it without wrapping the steamer lid. It will take almost twice as long to steam when covered with foil, but the texture will be firm and nice.

1½ cups all purpose flour
1 tsp. baking soda
½ tsp. salt
1 tsp. cinnamon
1 tsp. powdered ginger
¼ tsp. powdered cloves
½ cup brown sugar
1 egg, lightly beaten
½ cup molasses
½ cup vegetable oil
½ cup boiling water

Grease a 8x8-inch or other size heatproof baking pan that fits into steamer, or two small loaf pans. Start heating water in steamer. Combine flour, soda, salt, cinnamon, ginger and cloves. Stir in sugar, beaten egg and molasses. Add vegetable oil and boiling water and stir until smooth. Pour batter into prepared pan. Either cover baking pan with foil or wrap steamer lid with a dish towel to prevent mixture from dripping back onto cake.

When steamer water has come to a boil, place cake in steamer on a rack above water, cover steamer and steam. If steaming without foil, the cake will be done in about 20 to 25 minutes, or when an inserted knife blade comes out clean. If steaming cake with a foil cover, steam about 45 minutes, or until center of cake is firm to the touch and has risen slightly in the middle. Remove from steamer and allow to cool for several hours before serving.

GREEN CHILE CORNBREAD

Servings: 6-8

*This spicy bread is a family favorite. If you like really hot food, add a little chopped jalapeño, too. Should you have leftovers, crumble the cornbread and freeze it for use in **Savory Corn Pudding**, page 160.*

2 eggs
¼ cup vegetable oil
1 cup buttermilk
1 cup flour
1 cup yellow cornmeal
1 tbs. sugar

2 tsp. soda
½ tsp. salt
½ tsp. dry mustard
½ tsp. cumin
⅓ cup chopped canned green chiles, or to taste

Bring water to boil in steamer. Combine eggs, oil and buttermilk in a mixing bowl. Sift together flour, cornmeal, sugar, soda, salt, dry mustard and cumin. Add to eggs with green chiles. Just stir enough to combine. Spray an 8x8-inch pan or another heatproof dish that fits into steamer with nonstick cooking spray. Pour in cornbread batter. When steamer water boils, place pan on steamer tray, wrap lid of steamer in a dish towel so condensation doesn't drip into bread, cover and steam for 25 to 30 minutes, until a knife inserted into center comes out clean. Serve hot.

PUDDINGS AND CAKES

Puddings both sweet and savory are fun to do in the steamer. The *Tuna Pudding* and *Savory Corn Pudding* make delicious luncheon or supper entreés. Serve them right out of the heatproof cooking container with a green salad, or crudite, and some hot bread. The *Steamed Chocolate Cake, Orange Cake* and *Sweet Carrot Pudding* are very impressive when unmolded. These can be made ahead and served at room temperature, or refrigerated and warmed a little in the microwave just before serving. The *Cinnamon Bread Pudding*s are individual old-fashioned desserts steamed in custard cups.

For desserts that take long steaming times, check the water level in the steamer frequently, adding more boiling water when necessary.

TUNA PUDDING

Most people love tuna fish and this delicious pudding is definitely comfort food. It makes a great lunch or supper entrée.

2 tbs. butter
½ cup chopped onion
2 tbs. flour
1 cup milk
1 can (6½ oz.) tuna, drained
⅓ cup chopped green chiles

⅓ cup shredded sharp cheddar
  cheese
2 tbs. grated Parmesan cheese
3 eggs, lightly beaten
salt and freshly ground pepper

Melt butter in a medium saucepan and sauté onion 4 to 5 minutes until soft. Stir in flour and cook over low heat 2 minutes. Gradually add milk and cook until sauce thickens. Remove from heat; stir in tuna, green chiles, cheeses, eggs, salt and pepper. Spray a 5-cup heatproof dish with nonstick cooking spray and pour in tuna mixture. Cover with foil, crimping sides, and place in steamer. When steamer water comes to a boil, time pudding for 45 to 50 minutes, or until center of pudding is firm to the touch. Remove from steamer and serve immediately in a steaming dish.

SAVORY CORN PUDDING

This dish goes together quickly with items usually found in the cupboard. If you have some leftover cornbread, this is the perfect use for it. This is substantial enough to serve as a light entrée with a crisp green salad and some crunchy garlic bread.

3 eggs
2 tbs. vegetable oil
1 can (12 oz.) evaporated milk
1 tbs. sugar
½ tsp. salt
generous amount of white pepper

4-6 drops Tabasco Sauce, or to taste
1 cup creamed canned corn
¼ cup diced ham, diced green
  chiles, or pimiento, optional
dash paprika

Beat eggs, and add oil, milk, sugar, salt, pepper and Tabasco. Stir in corn and ham. Spray a 5-cup heatproof baking dish with nonstick cooking spray and pour egg mixture into dish. Spray one side of a piece of aluminum foil with nonstick cooking spray and place oil-side down over baking dish, crimping sides to keep out steam. When steamer water comes to a boil, place baking dish on a steaming rack and place in steamer. Steam covered for 45 minutes. Carefully uncover, sprinkle with paprika, and serve immediately in steaming dish.

STEAMED CHOCOLATE CAKE

Servings: 10-12

Serve this tender chocolate cake with a custard sauce, good vanilla ice cream or fresh raspberries and cream.

3 oz. unsweetened chocolate
½ cup butter
2 eggs
1 cup brown sugar
2 tsp. vanilla
1 cup buttermilk
2 cups flour
2 tsp. baking soda
1 tsp. baking powder
½ tsp. salt

Generously butter a 2-quart bowl or steaming mold that will fit into steamer. Place a small rack in bottom of steamer so water can circulate. Water should come halfway up side of mold. Melt chocolate and butter together and allow to cool slightly. Beat together eggs, sugar, vanilla and buttermilk. Add chocolate.

Sift together dry ingredients and add to egg mixture. Spoon into prepared mold.

Tightly cover mold with two pieces of aluminum foil and tie with a string. When steamer water comes to a boil, place mold in steamer on rack, cover and lower heat so water is gently boiling. Steam for 1½ hours. Cake will spring back to the touch, and a knife blade should come out clean when cake is done. Carefully remove mold from steamer and allow to rest for at least 10 minutes before unmolding. If not serving warm, invert mold over cake to retain some of the moisture while it is cooling. Cut into slices to serve. Serve with ice cream or a vanilla sauce.

STEAMED ORANGE CAKE

Servings: 10-12

This is a bright moist orange-flavored cake, drenched with lemon and orange juice while it is still hot.

½ cup butter
1 cup sugar
2 eggs
¼ cup concentrated orange juice, defrosted
2 tsp. vanilla
1 tbs. Triple Sec or Grand Marnier
⅔ cup milk
1¾ cups flour
3 tbs. baking powder
½ tsp. salt

Generously butter a 2-quart bowl or steaming mold that will fit into steamer. Place a small rack in bottom of steamer so water can circulate. Water should come halfway up side of mold. Bring steamer water to a boil.

Beat together butter and sugar; add eggs, mixing well. Add orange juice, vanilla, Triple Sec and milk. Sift dry ingredients together and add to egg mixture. Spoon into prepared mold. Tightly cover mold with a double thickness of aluminum foil and tie with a string. When water comes to a boil, place mold in steamer on rack, cover and steam for 1½ hours. Lower heat so water is gently boiling. Cake will spring back to the touch, and a knife blade should come out clean when cake is done. Carefully remove mold from steamer and allow to rest for at least 10 minutes before unmolding. With a skewer or cake tester, poke holes into cake and pour *Orange Lemon Sauce* over cake while it is still warm.

ORANGE LEMON SAUCE
¾ cup sifted powdered sugar
rind from 1 orange
2 tbs. lemon juice
2 tbs. orange juice

   Combine ingredients.

SWEET CARROT PUDDING

Servings: 10-12

This dense, spicy pudding will remind you of a terrific carrot cake.

3 large eggs
1 cup sugar
⅓ cup vegetable oil
1½ cups finely grated carrots
½ cup applesauce
2 tbs. lemon juice
1½ cups flour
1 tsp. baking powder

2 tsp. baking soda
1 tsp. salt
1 tsp. cinnamon
¼ tsp. powdered ginger
¼ tsp. cloves
½ tsp. allspice
1 cup raisins, light or dark
½ cup chopped walnuts

Beat eggs well. Add sugar and oil. Add carrots, applesauce and lemon juice. Sift flour with baking power, soda, salt and spices. Add to egg mixture and stir in raisins and walnuts. Spoon into a well-buttered 2-quart bowl or mold that will fit into steamer. Tightly cover mold with two pieces of aluminum foil and tie with a string. When water comes to a boil, place mold in steamer on rack, cover and steam for 1¾ hours. Water should come halfway up side of mold. Lower heat so water is gently boiling. Pudding will spring back to the touch, will be slightly puffed in center, and a knife blade will come out clean when pudding is done. Carefully remove mold from steamer and allow to rest for at least 10 minutes before unmolding. Serve with whipped cream, if desired.

CINNAMON BREAD PUDDING

Servings: 4

This old-fashioned dessert makes a perfect not-too-sweet ending for a hearty soup or stew dinner.

2 eggs
1/3 cup heavy cream
2 tbs. brown sugar
1½ cups cubed day-old bread

½ tsp. cinnamon
dash nutmeg
1 tbs. brandy or rum
¼ cup raisins

Beat eggs and combine with remaining ingredients. Spray four 5 to 6 oz. custard cups with nonstick cooking spray and spoon mixture into cups. Cover cups with a piece of foil, crimping foil around edges. Place a steamer rack in bottom of the steamer. When steamer water comes to a boil, carefully place pudding cups on rack, cover steamer and steam for 20 minutes. Puddings are done when a knife blade comes out clean or pudding is lightly puffed in the middle. Serve warm or at room temperature.

STACKED STEAMER MEALS

Steaming is a very efficient method for cooking several different dishes at the same time, and it is easy to put together a complete delicious dinner by using two or three steamer baskets. Large aluminum steamers with two or three steamer baskets, or a set of two or three bamboo baskets with a lid, or electric steamers with stackable baskets will work best for multiple steaming operations. There must be enough room left around the plates or bowls to allow the steam to circulate freely. Food placed closest to the boiling water cooks the fastest, so the longer cooking dishes should be placed on the first layer. The second steamer layer will require a little additional steamer time and a third layer another extra 5 minutes. The steamer baskets can be switched halfway during the cooking to even out the cooking time.

Here are some suggested menus for stacked steamer meals, and you can put together your own favorite combinations from other sections of this book.

CHINESE SPECIAL DINNER
Steamed Asparagus or Broccoli
Eggplant with Plum Sauce
Reheated cooked rice

SHORE DINNER
Steamed Lobster, Steamed Clams
Steamed Potatoes and Sweet Corn

WINTER EVENING SPECIAL
Belgian Beef Stew
Steamed Cabbage and New Potatoes

SALMON SALAD NIÇOISE
Steamed Salmon
Steamed New Potatoes
Hard Boiled Eggs
Green Beans

DIM SUM LUNCHEON
Shrimp and Scallop Shao Mai
Paper Wrapped Salmon
Steamed Duck Buns
Steamed Beef Cilantro Balls

APRÈS SKI SUPPER
Brisket Mexicana
Steamer Polenta

CURRY DINNER
Curried Chicken Thighs
Steamed Rice
Steamed Gingered Oranges or
   Chunky Apple Sauce

QUICK AND EASY
Chicken Breasts Milano
Green Beans
Pears in Red Wine

BRUNCH FAVORITES
Dried Fruit Compote
Crustless Onion Quiche
Pumpkin Nut Bread

CALIFORNIA BOUNTY
Steamed Crab with Easy Mayonnaise
Artichokes

STEAM-IT-AHEAD BUFFET STARS
Seafood Terrine
Turkey Breast Stuffed with
  Goat Cheese and Peppers
Duck and Lentil Salad
Peaches with Raspberries

KITCHEN PARTY
Spinach-Stuffed Mushrooms
Chile Verde with Tortillas
Spicy Orange-Flavored Apples

GARDEN TREASURES
Savory Swiss Chard Bundles
Zucchini-Yellow Squash Combo

COCKTAIL PARTY MENU
Eggplant Sesame Dip
Spaghetti Squash Frittata
Salmon-Stuffed Grape Leaves

FISHERMAN'S CATCH
Stuffed Trout
Potato Vegetable Combo

MIDDLE EASTERN DELIGHTS
Turkish-Style Stuffed Eggplants
Couscous
Cauliflower Calcutta

DO-AHEAD PICNIC
Mexican-Style Fish Salad
Russian Vegetable Salad
Applesauce Apricot Bread

INDEX

SERVE CREATIVE, EASY, NUTRITIOUS MEALS WITH NITTY GRITTY® COOKBOOKS

Convection Oven Cookery
The Steamer Cookbook
The Pasta Machine Cookbook
The Versatile Rice Cooker
The Dehydrator Cookbook
Waffles
The Coffee Book
The Bread Machine Cookbook
The Bread Machine Cookbook II
The Bread Machine Cookbook III
The Bread Machine Cookbook IV
The Sandwich Maker Cookbook
The Juicer Book
The Juicer Book II
Bread Baking (traditional),
  revised
The Kid's Cookbook, revised

Quick & Easy Pasta Recipes,
  revised
15-Minute Meals for 1 or 2
Recipes for the 9x13 Pan
Extra-Special Crockery Pot
  Recipes
Chocolate Cherry Tortes and
  Other Lowfat Delights
Lowfat American Favorites
Lowfat International Cuisine
The Hunk Cookbook
Now That's Italian!
Fabulous Fiber Cookery
Low Salt, Low Sugar, Low Fat
  Desserts
Healthy Cooking on the Run
Healthy Snacks for Kids

Creative Soups & Salads
Muffins, Nut Breads and More
The Barbecue Book
The Wok
Quiche & Soufflé Cookbook
Cooking for 1 or 2
New Ways to Enjoy Chicken
Favorite Seafood Recipes
No Salt, No Sugar, No Fat
  Cookbook
New International Fondue
  Cookbook
Favorite Cookie Recipes
Authentic Mexican Cooking
Fisherman's Wharf Cookbook
The Creative Lunch Box

Write or call for our free catalog.
Bristol Publishing Enterprises, Inc.
P.O. Box 1737, San Leandro, CA 94577
(800)346-4889; in California (510)895-4461